Faith at Work

Peter H. Michell

New Wine Press

New Wine Press
PO Box 17
Chichester
West Sussex PO20 6YB
England

ISBN 1 874367 25 6

Typeset by CRB (Drayton) Typesetting Services, Drayton, Norwich
Printed in England by Clays Ltd, St Ives plc.

Contents

Foreword

A few years ago I visited Israel for the first time and, with my wife, found myself in the Garden Tomb in Jerusalem – the site many believe to be that from which Jesus rose from the dead.

The peace and beauty and the awesome sense of His presence in this sanctuary contrasts with the smell of diesel fumes, the noise of bus engines and car hooters and of market traders vying for business immediately outside the Garden.

Beneath the place where Jesus was crucified – Golgotha – there is a bus station. The area is the heart of commercial life in East Jerusalem. I found the contrast overwhelming – my pre-conceptions were shattered! Jamie Buckingham in his book *The Nazarene* (Kingsway) asks of this contrast 'Is that a sacrilege?' and answers 'I think not. Rather it seems providential' and he quotes an unknown author who put it this way:

> 'I simply argue that the Cross be raised again at the centre of the market-place as well as on the steeple of the church. I am recovering the claim that Jesus was not crucified in a cathedral between two candles, but on a rugged cross between two thieves on a town garbage heap; at the crossroads of politics so cosmopolitan that they had to write His title in Hebrew and in Latin and in Greek ... And at a kind of place where cynics talk smut, and thieves curse and soldiers gamble. Because that is

where He died, Golgotha's tree; and that is what He
died about.

It is there where Christ's men ought to be, and what
church people ought to be about.'

It is from 'there' – in the harsh, noisy and, yes, frequently
smelly, cheap and greedy market-place – that Peter Michell
has written. I commend this book to you most warmly,
believing it to be deeply challenging to all called to work out
our walk of faith in the market-place.

For far too many years I worked in my job as a chartered
surveyor having little concept of the implications of God
having 'called' me to the commercial world; indeed, if I had
been totally honest, I would have said that I felt a second-
class Christian. The 'real' men and women of faith were
those fulfilling 'full-time' ministries, such as ministers in the
Church, evangelists, missionaries and the like. By being in
the market-place I was somehow a part of the world, of that
world that surrounds the Garden Tomb – a world of much
that shouts against the gospel of Christ as I understood it.

Peter Michell challenges us to recognise that a calling into
the business and political realms of society is as significant as
any 'full-time' service; indeed it *is* full-time service. God
loves the economy; it is the life-blood of a nation and supports all other realms of society – home and family, education, medical care, law and order, the media, politics and
recreation.

It is Satan and his hosts that have led many Christians in
business to view their jobs as second-best. In so doing he has
successfully undermined our expectancy of God intervening
in our work situations. The truth is that we are called to be in
the world but not of it, to be ambassadors for Christ wherever we are.

Peter Michell has a testimony to the Lord's transforming,
intervening power and of the authority that He has given to
those who have surrendered their lives to Him, as Saviour
and Lord. Jesus demonstrated the reality of the Kingdom of
God through His daily life, and He told the disciples who
came from John the Baptist enquiring as to whether He was

'the Coming One' – *'Go and tell John the things you have seen and heard.'* The world of commerce and politics urgently needs to *see* and hear through the lives of our Lord's disciples called to the market-place. We have a responsibility to work out our high calling, that the world may again *see* the difference *'between the righteous and the wicked, between one who serves God and one who does not serve Him'* (Malachi 3:18).

The days are urgent. Never has the message brought to us in this book been more needed. The time to stand as believers, trusting Him who called us, is **now**. The world is looking for answers as the shaking of the nations intensifies; and Jesus is looking to you and to me – as those whom He has redeemed – to go in the anointing of the Holy Spirit; to take the ministry we have been given, to see sick businesses healed in His Name, dead business lives raised to life and demonic powers put to flight as you and I take our positions.

I am privileged to have known Peter Michell over many years and to have been actively involved, as he has been, in the ministry of the Full Gospel Businessmens Fellowship International (FGBMFI). Over the past five years we have also worked together in the International Christian Chamber of Commerce (ICCC), a complementary ministry to that of the FGBMFI and which is supporting the publication and distribution of this timely book.

In highly commending *Faith at Work* to you, I trust that you will be so challenged by it that your life in the market-place will be transformed and that your light may *'so shine before men, that they may see your good works and glorify your Father in heaven'* (Matthew 5:16).

Michael Fenton-Jones

Michael Fenton-Jones is a Chartered Surveyor, recently retired non-executive Chairman of the Commercial Union Assurance Group's property 'arm' (Commercial Union Properties Ltd), Property Adviser to British Airways plc and a director of a number of property related companies.

He is Vice-President of the International Christian Chamber of Commerce and Chairman of the UK Board (known in the UK as the Council of Christians in Commerce Ltd).

Introduction

'The bank has demanded repayment of the company's overdraft and we can't pay. We've tried several other banks to no avail, so we've decided to liquidate and I need some advice – the bank is going to take the house!'

John's words were all too familiar. But John was a Christian. What was wrong? Why do so many of God's children struggle and fail? It can't be God's will, can it?

I cast my mind back to just over a year ago when John was in my office telling me of this new business he had just started with another chap. He told me of his 'vision' – a Christian school. After all there is great need to provide Christian education for our young folk and this business was going to make good profits and finance the school.

John was an expert in his field, and recognised as such, and the market was an expanding market. He had produced a very credible business plan and obtained an overdraft from his bank. All he needed from me was advice on how to set up and run a simple accounting system and comply with all the regulations – Income Tax, VAT and the like.

In that first interview, after answering all John's questions, I had a few of my own. Did God tell you to start this business? How did He say that to you? Are you sure? What other witness was there? John answered my questions and left full of enthusiasm for his venture. I was left with a strong sense of foreboding – he hadn't been able to answer my questions in any specific way and didn't seem able to hear me when I warned him of the consequences of starting out without instructions from his heavenly Father.

So now here we were picking up the pieces.

Just a couple of years before I had seen a number of Christian businessmen fail – they were all in one local church and set on building the Kingdom – their businesses were going to finance God's work. Regular prayer meetings were the order of the day, the support of the elders, lots of enthusiasm. Not one survived. They all failed.

By the grace of God, I have come to realise that there are principles by which we will succeed or fail. Those principles apply to the whole of life including our working lives. In this book I have tried to share my understanding illustrating it with examples from work and life in general on the basis that we won't succeed at work if we fail at home.

Whether the challenge is a business with a huge cash flow problem, or, how to catch a recalcitrant horse, or, a bank manager with a bad attitude, or, whatever – the Lord knows the answer. Part of our calling is to **reign in life** as we receive the abundance of grace and the gift of righteousness according to Romans 5:17.

The Lord has led me through experiences of my own which have taught me principles to apply in business (as well as the rest of my Christian life) but I didn't know anyone else experiencing the same learning curve. Then, a few years ago, I was introduced to the International Christian Chamber of Commerce and I discovered that there were others who had walked the same path and learnt the same lessons.

After a little while I became involved in the teaching ministry of ICCC – hence this book. I'm sure it is not complete and that there is more to learn and appreciate, but in the meantime here are the lessons I have learnt from both my own experience and from observing many others, some clients, some friends and some both.

I do hope that this book will help and inspire you to walk even more in the abundance of grace with the result that you reign in life more and more.

Chapter 1

A Contract Has Been Entered

'I want you to give Me your life.' The voice was warm and encouraging, sort of compelling without being hard or force-ful. It was my decision, and I couldn't refuse.

'Yes Lord Jesus, I give You my life, please come in.' I was seventeen and in an evangelistic meeting in Hertfordshire. The sermon, a call to salvation, was being given by the minister of the Baptist church I had attended for a few months. We (the youth) were holding a crusade in a small church about 40 miles from home.

But it wasn't the minister I heard speaking to me, neither could I see him, though he was only a few feet away. This was something new to me; I was receiving a spiritual experi-ence and the voice was the voice of Jesus. I was entering into a contract.

For His part, He was offering to take the penalty of my sin, to wash me clean and to give me His righteousness. He had earned the right to make me the offer through His death on the cross, where, according to Isaiah, He rendered Him-self as a guilt offering and was pierced for my transgressions, crushed for my iniquitites (Isaiah 53).

God was demonstrating His love toward me in that whilst I was a sinner, Christ had died for me (Romans 5:8). Instead of being paid the wages of sin – death – I was now receiving the free gift from God – eternal life, in Christ Jesus my Lord (Romans 6:23).

For my part I had nothing of any note to offer Him in exchange. I gave Him my sin and failure.

When I said 'Yes Lord, come in,' the contract was completed. He took me at my word. He came in and I was sealed in Him with the Holy Spirit of promise (Ephesians 1:13).

Not that I understood the full meaning of what was happening, neither did I know the full extent of it as revealed in the Scripture. My understanding has grown and is still growing as time goes on.

Everyone's experience of being born again is different. Chris, John and Douglas have shared their experiences in the testimonies at the end of the book.

Bought with a price

However, the contract was not cheap from His point of view – it cost Him His life on earth, it cost Him an agonising death on the cross, it cost Him shame and nakedness as mankind crucified Him. I had been bought with a price.

> *'You are not your own ... you have been bought with a price.'*   (1 Corinthians 6:19, 20)

He made His payment in full, did everything necessary to fulfil His part of the contract. He knew me from the start and knew my intentions and abilities. He also knew that I would fail many times in the days to come. Yet knowing all this He made the offer and He took me on.

Born again

Now I knew by experience the meaning of the statement 'born again'. A learned teacher and religious ruler of Jesus' day named Nicodemus came to Jesus by night. Jesus said to him,

> *'Truly, truly I say to you, unless one is born again, he cannot see the Kingdom of God.'*   (John 3:3)

By way of further explanation He added,

> '*Truly, truly, I say to you, unless one is born of water and the Spirit, he cannot enter into the Kingdom of God. That which is born of flesh is flesh, and that which is born of the Spirit is spirit.*' (John 3:5–6)

The Scripture declares that we all died in Adam, a reference to death of the spirit of man; and further declares that in Christ we are made alive.

This was my time to be born again – I didn't understand my experience at the time. I knew I had committed my life to Jesus and the understanding followed as I learnt through others and the Scripture.

Being born again is not a question of doing or being good. Rather it is a question of receiving through God's grace the provision of salvation and the life-restoring touch of the Holy Spirit. The Holy Spirit brings new life to the spirit of man which otherwise dwells in the kingdom of death and darkness.

Going my own way

After the initial experience of being born again I concentrated on my studies. I was articled to a Chartered Accountant in the West End of London.

I married (later we had three children), qualified and duly 'set out' on a career path. After qualifying I was offered a job in industry as accountant to a small manufacturing company. The company grew and we prospered as a family.

I became interested in the commercial aspect of business and when the opportunity came to be appointed as Managing Director of a new venture being started by the company I was working for, I grabbed it.

We found an empty factory, purchased equipment and started manufacturing our new products. After four years the company I was running was selling over £1m of its products and making about £100,000 per annum in profits. Not at all bad back in the 1970s.

However, I had not even considered whether I was

fulfilling God's will for my life when abruptly the job came to an end! I had a severe disagreement with the chairman (and owner) of the parent company and left the same day.

Built on sand

My life was on sand. We had, just a few months before, bought a new house, with what was then a huge mortgage, and just started our son at public school. Expenses were at an all-time high. You know the type of decision we make – 'it will be a bit of a strain at first but after a year or so, with a rise, it will work out.' We were straining our finances to step up in the world. Crash! Record expenses and no income.

The contract of love

There were a number of things I had not appreciated at that time, but which I have come to appreciate now that I have experienced more of life as a born-again Christian.

Firstly, the contract I had entered into with Jesus was a contract of love.

> *'God so loved the world that He gave His only begotten Son, that whosoever believes in Him should not perish but have eternal life.'* (John 3:16)

Secondly, God actually has desires and plans for my life.

> *'"For I know the plans that I have for you," declares the Lord, "plans for welfare and not for calamity to give you a future and a hope."'* (Jeremiah 29:11)

In my ignorance I didn't know that love was a matter of choice. In fact, whilst I pursued **my** career, I lost sight of God as my loving Father who wanted my love in return. I had to learn that the object of life was not **my** career but that He had all rights over my life, having bought me with a price, and He had a chosen pathway for me.

Out of work

I was 'between jobs', as we would now say, for six months. It was a period of greatly mixed blessings. On the one hand I started to read the Bible and books by Spirit-inspired authors. These generated in me an understanding that God loved me, was interested in the detail and direction of my life, and was able to intervene on my behalf. On the other hand all our financial reserves were draining away!

In fact the problem of finance was becoming a major worry as the time went on. Not that we lacked anything during the period of unemployment, but rather that it appeared as though we were going over the financial edge and into the abyss.

That's when I heard God speak again, not about direction for work or life but a simple statement which met my point of need. 'Peter, do not worry about money. I will look after you.' There was no explanation of how or when, just 'Trust Me.'

I had heard from God: maybe it was an audible voice or maybe not, I don't actually know. What I do know is that God Himself spoke to me. The result was a transformation of my thinking. Money is not my problem. Providing for my family is not my problem. Why? Because God has told me to trust Him.

The choice of love

Now I was beginning to appreciate what it means to be loved by God and to love Him. In terms of understanding I now appreciate far better the meaning of the Scripture.

There are two words in the Greek text, both translated as 'love' in our English versions.

'*Agape*' means 'to choose to consider the one loved more important than oneself'. There is emphasis on the element of choice, so *agape* means to choose to love.

'*Phileo*' means friendship love. The natural easy-going good feeling towards someone which develops into deep friendship.

I found that the contract I had entered into with Jesus had

a lot to say about love. In fact, love was the most important clause of all. That God loved me had become both knowledge and experience. Not a once and for all thing, but a new life that started when I was born-again and is still developing in richness and depth day by day. His love for me couldn't be called into question – He had given His life for me – He has wonderful plans for my life.

The problem was my love for Him. In the early days it was pathetic to say the least. In fact, it wasn't until my own efforts at making a way in life had failed and I was out of work, that there was any real progress. However, the Lord knows our weaknesses and He comes to lead us to the point where our relationship with Him is perfected step by step.

Then I began to get understanding: I could **choose** to love Jesus. This is what the scripture meant, when God said:

> *'love the Lord your God with all your heart, and with all your soul and with all your mind.'* (Matthew 22:37)

It meant that I could choose to do just that.

In fact, one day I was kneeling at my bed praying, saying to Jesus 'I love You,' when I felt a rebuke. It was as if He were saying back, 'No you don't.' I immediately understood where I was – my words were from my intellect but my heart was not fully and completely in love with Him.

'Sorry Lord, please forgive me and please, Holy Spirit, fill me with more and more love for Jesus.' Then it became a regular prayer, 'Holy Spirit please fill me with more and more love for Jesus.' I would like to commend this prayer to you for I have found that my relationship with Jesus has become the most valuable part of all of life by far.

Looking at the Scripture I found that God had committed Himself to love me, both as His friend and by His choice. It was His *'agape'* for me which caused the Father to allow Jesus to go to the cross and that Jesus is the lover of mankind (from *'phileo'*) is found in Titus 3:4.

I also discovered that God expected me to love Him both by choice and by friendship. The command to love the Lord

with all your heart, soul and mind is *'agape'*. In 1 Corinthians 16:22 is the statement *'if anyone does not love* ('phileo') *the Lord, let him be accursed.'*

The contract – love based

So there we have it. This contract by which Jesus bought me is a contract of love. His intention towards me is always good. Jesus knows me better than I know myself, and He therefore knows what is best for me better than I do. Simple logic requires that I relax in the knowledge that this contract is the best and most wonderful contract I will ever enter.

The contract is a wonderful expression of God's love. He has bound Himself by its terms. As a businessman, I know that, in order to benefit from a contract, one must abide by and fulfil its terms. In the contract of love with the Lord, He has allowed for our failures. In a normal contract our failure would result in the loss of the benefit. In this contract God allows for our failures and yet is Himself still bound by the terms.

Building on rock instead

In the parable in Matthew 7 recorded from verse 24 to the end of the chapter, two builders both hear the word of God. The wise builder hears the words of God and acts upon them – he builds on rock. The foolish builder hears the words of God and ignores them – he builds on the sand.

Building on the rock is always going to be a harder task than building on sand but the reward is shown in the parable. The storm hits both buildings. We are not exempt from the storms; the question is whether we will stand or fall as a consequence of our foundations.

So I started to build on rock by applying the words of God to my own life. It is harder than building on sand because my own desires (what the Scripture describes as 'the flesh') have to be crucified. My own thinking has to change.

The process actually becomes easier the more I love Jesus and continues to be easier the more I am focused on Him.

The benefits became apparent. I am discovering that His plan for my life is better than my own ideas and plans.

Bought with a price that was paid

Although God could demand that we fulfil the contract, He waits and gently leads us towards Himself step by step. Sometimes we advance in giant steps forward and sometimes in small ones, but all the time He wants us to come closer and closer in our experience of Himself.

My business instincts tell me that God is not like others who enter into contracts. He could insist on my compliance. He doesn't – He waits, loves, draws me to Himself. However, I can now see that to ignore the contract, or to rebel against Him in any way, is sheer folly, for He loves me more than I can comprehend. What I need is wisdom...

Chapter 2

Wisdom is What I Need

We come to consider a most fundamental question for all Christians and a question which will have substantial effect on our working life:

What 'wisdom' is available to assist and guide me?

The terms of the contract

'You are not your own ... you have been bought with a price.' (1 Corinthians 6:20)

I no longer belong to me. Actually, my desires and wishes should no longer be the driving force of my life, because ownership has changed.

God does not enforce His rights but, nevertheless, those rights exist. I did discover and will discover, that all the time I am following my own way, problems abound. In fact, problems abound anyway. What changes is that, as I follow Him, He comes to my assistance and changes the circumstances.

Straightforward logic would dictate that you cannot expect God to come to your assistance in any given situation if you are not in relationship with Him, following His leading.

When I was following my own ambitions my business life prospered for a while, but then overnight it fell apart and I found myself unemployed. God could not 'save' the position because I had walked out of His purposes for my life. Whilst

I walked after my own desires and my own direction God allowed the circumstances of failure so that I would stop and take stock.

Ephesians 2:10 says that,

> *'For we are His workmanship, created in Christ Jesus for good works, which God prepared beforehand, that we should walk in them.'*

God has a specific purpose for you

He has prepared good works for you and me to walk in. My problem was that I took no notice of the Scripture or of the Spirit of God in the decision to change my job.

I **wanted** to be managing director of the plastics engineering business, regardless of what God might say or want. I could excuse myself, by saying that I didn't really understand then that God had a plan for me. But I think probably the truth is that, even if I had known, I would still have gone my own way.

Paul speaks to the Corinthians in chapter 7 of his first letter. He is actually advising about marriage and in so doing he relates some very wise advice:

> *'Only as the Lord has assigned to each one, as God has called each, in this manner let him walk.'* (v. 17)

> *'Let each man remain in that condition in which he was called.'* (v. 20)

I had missed it. When I was called – that is called by Jesus to give my life to Him – I was an accountancy student. He blessed me in that and enabled me to understand adequately the subject to qualify when I was only twenty-one. As an accountant my work went well and my income rose quickly.

Why did I change from accountancy to general management? Simply, because I found accountancy dull, and I was excited by the concept and practice of running a business.

In so doing I fell foul of God's declared will for my life. For His scripture above declares that I should stay in the calling in which I was called. That does not mean that a change is not possible. However, we should wait for Him to tell us to change and not go our own way. I was acting as if God had not bought me with a price.

The fear of the Lord is the beginning of wisdom

> *'To know wisdom and instruction, to discern the sayings of understanding, to receive instruction in wise behaviour, righteousness, justice and equity, to give prudence to the naive, to the youth knowledge and discretion. A wise man will hear and increase in learning, and a man of understanding will acquire wise counsel.'*
>
> (Proverbs 1:2–5)

> *'The fear of the Lord is the beginning of knowledge. Fools despise wisdom and instruction.'*   (Proverbs 1:7)

A new business philosophy

The dictionary describes the meaning of 'philosophy' as:

> 'seeking after wisdom and knowledge' or 'system of principles for the conduct of life.'

We fairly readily apply scriptural principles to life in general but somehow Monday morning is a different matter – it's business or work and we often apply different rules.

It's as if we think God is not interested, or perhaps not able, to have any effect in the realm of our working lives.

It's time to realise that God is not only interested, but has specific plans. Not only is He able to change situations in our working lives and environment, but also He wants to and will.

The promises of wisdom

> *'How blessed is the man who finds wisdom and the man who gains understanding.*

> *For its profit is better than the profit of silver and its gain than fine gold.'* (Proverbs 3:13–14)

As a businessman I find the above verses appealing. I want to be blessed and I want profit and if there is better profit than just money I want that as well.

God's wisdom is beneficial

The book of Proverbs is full of the benefits of wisdom, here are a few from chapters 2 and 3:

> *'Favour and good repute with God and man.'*
> *'Straightening of my path.'*
> *'Healing to my body.'*
> *'Refreshment.'*
> *'Long life.'*
> *'Peace and happiness.'*
> *'Security and confidence.'*
> *'Increase in knowledge.'*

There are many times in business when I need favour with man and I have learnt to ask God to grant that favour. Sitting in front of a difficult tax inspector or a bank manager with a client is a case in point.

Often my path needs straightening:

Sally was upset. Obviously what she was going to tell me was difficult for her. So here we were in my office first thing in the morning. Sally was working for me part-time as a book-keeper.

'Peter, I don't know how to tell you this, but I've taken a full-time job in London. How are you going to manage? I'm so sorry but I've got to take it.'

Sally was not a believer although she had heard me talk about Jesus from time to time, so my reply was probably not too strange to her ears. 'Don't worry Sally, the Lord will provide for me. You carry on with no concern, be blessed and prosper.'

The little red light on the ansaphone was flashing to indicate that after hours yesterday a 'phone call had come in and been recorded, so I flicked the switch to hear the message. My office is open plan and the ansaphone fairly loud, so Sally and the others could also hear:

'You don't know me, my name is Lesley and I think you might be looking for a book-keeper, my number is...'

We were all rather taken aback, the answer was there even before we knew the need. *'Before you call I will answer.'* Sally was stunned. God acts.

It was rather like a time a couple of years previously, when there was just me and a part-time secretary. Work was piling up; we were getting more and more new clients.

'How are you going to cope with all this work, Peter?' was Kathy's question one day.

'God will provide some help' was my reply.

Kathy is a believer so had no problem with the concept, but would He in practice do anything?

The same day, a couple of hours later, an accountant acquaintance 'phoned me. 'Peter, I've got a chap here studying for his accountancy exams and he needs some work, have you anything you can give him?'

Where does wisdom point us?

Matthew has it in chapter 6:33:

> *'Seek first His kingdom and His righteousness and all these things will be added to you.'*

These things, in context, are food and clothing and described as the things the Gentiles seek after. We can apply the principle to any area of need.

Seek His kingdom

What does it mean to seek His kingdom? Well my understanding is this: a kingdom is somewhere where the king has power and influence, where the king reigns. So for me to seek His kingdom, is to seek His rulership over my life, not to do my own will but to align my will with His.

And His righteousness

Righteousness is a gift from God, given at the point of salvation.

> *'For if by the transgression of the one, death reigned through the one, much more those who receive the abundance of grace and of the gift of righteousness will reign in life through the One, Christ Jesus.'*
>
> (Romans 5:17)

I had received His righteousness. To be true to the righteousness that I had received, the word requires that I should obey His commandments, that I should be righteous in all my ways. I'm still working on that and so is the Holy Spirit who continues to change me.

One key which I have come to understand is this:

> *'If you love me you will obey my commandments.'*
>
> (John 14:15)

Imagine this in picture format. Think of a horse and cart – the horse comes first, pulling the cart.

Loving Jesus is the horse and obeying His commands is the cart that follows. What I am saying, is that the more one loves the Lord, the more one obeys His commands. So my frequent prayer to the Holy Spirit, 'fill me with more love for Jesus' is actually also bringing about a more righteous walk with Him.

It is very easy to place the cart before the horse. In many scriptures the Spirit talks about righteous behaviour. However, if we focus on our behaviour, we can become legalistic. The Old Covenant was not given for the Jews to obey to the letter; it was given as a tutor to lead to Christ. The point is this, God's standards are so high that no one can keep them. It is inevitable that you and I will fail. Therefore we need a redeemer, someone to pay the penalty of our sin. Jesus does that and gives us His righteousness.

The more one considers this, the more one realises that one enemy of our relationship with God is legalism. The Law was ineffective in saving people – in fact, it was there not as a method of being saved but as a pointer to the need for a saviour. Not one jot or tittle has passed away from the Law. It still points out the need for a saviour.

If one focuses on being exactly right, the result is not an improvement in our relationship with God. We are to focus on Him, love Him with all our heart, all our soul and all our mind, to repent of our failures and co-operate with being changed by the Holy Spirit. The result will be that the desire to obey Him will be written in our hearts and our actions will become more Christ-like over a period of time.

New business philosophy

I hope it has become clear that a new philosophy is needed in the work realm: a philosophy which acknowledges that we were bought with a price, which sees that God has a particular plan for each one and a philosophy which says 'His ways are better than mine.' A philosophy which applies wisdom.

I have heard wisdom defined as the possession of knowledge with the practical ability to apply it. We certainly need to know and to apply that which is right in God's eyes.

So far so good, but what about my motives...?

Chapter 3

Motive

Introducing a new motive

Profit is frequently seen as 'the motive' for the businessman and generally speaking that is a fair view for the man of the world. However, the issue of motive is more complex than profit alone. Power, and influence and ambition are also strong motives at work in the market-place.

In chapter 4:13–16 James has something to say to businessmen:

> 'Come now you who say, today or tomorrow, we shall go to such and such a city, spend a year there and engage in business and make a profit. Yet you do not know what your life will be like tomorrow. You are just a vapour that appears for a little while and then vanishes away. Instead you ought to say, If the Lord wills, we shall live and do this or that. But as it is, you boast in your arrogance, all such boasting is evil.'

This passage actually confirms what we have already seen, that there is a way for us to follow – the good works that God has prepared beforehand and not our own good works.

James is saying that we ought to be submitted to the will of the Lord and not 'boasting' about what we are going to do. He is not making a comment on profit.

The profit motive

In fact, the Scripture strongly supports a free market economy in its approach to business matters (with the proviso that it also strongly supports the giving of help to the poor and needy as well as moral excellence in the ethics of business).

Consider the parable of the talents recorded by Matthew in chapter 25:14–30. The servants are given money and expected to trade with that money and produce a profit. Those servants who succeed are met with, *'well done good and faithful'*, whilst the one who did not even try is told, *'you wicked lazy slave'*, and then thrown into darkness.

There were three servants in the parable who were given five, two and one talents respectively. It is my understanding that every Christian has a minimum of two talents. My reasoning for this is as follows:

The gift of life itself is one talent given to everybody, believer or not. The unbeliever absolutely wastes that life, in effect digging it into the ground. The believer receives a second talent when he is born again, a gift of new life now in Jesus Christ. Actually, the believer is 'trading' with that talent just by being a believer in an unsaved world. Some believers trade more actively and some seem to receive more talents.

The fruitful kingdom

One of the main principles of the kingdom is that of fruitfulness.

> *'And God blessed them and God said to them, Be fruitful and multiply, and fill the earth, and subdue it.'*
>
> (Genesis 1:28)

> *'You did not choose Me, but I chose you, and appointed you that you should go and bear fruit.'*   (John 15:16)

The parable of the sower where the seed brings forth thirty, sixty and a hundred fold also points to the expectation of fruitfulness and growth.

The problem is not money

Money in itself is not a problem. Indeed money is an extremely useful medium of exchange which facilitates the transfer of goods and services between a multitude of people. But problems arise when money becomes an object of love.

> *'For the love of money is a root of all sorts of evil, and some by longing for it have wandered away from the faith, and pierced themselves with many a pang.'*
>
> (1 Timothy 6:10)

Love of money is a snare. *'You cannot serve God and mammon'* is Luke (16:13) and Matthew's (6:24) statement given in strong terms – you will love one and hate the other. One of the aspects of the love of money is that it brings self-inflicted pain and trouble.

So many people in the last few years, seeing prices rising rapidly, bought houses with a motive of gain, or greater gain, rather than what was necessary to meet just their needs. Now, as house prices have fallen just as swiftly, they face self-inflicted pain.

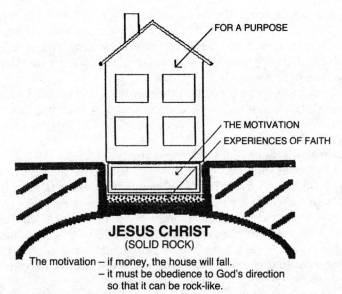

FOR A PURPOSE

THE MOTIVATION
EXPERIENCES OF FAITH

JESUS CHRIST
(SOLID ROCK)

The motivation – if money, the house will fall.
 – it must be obedience to God's direction so that it can be rock-like.

(Thanks to Jan Sturresson, Chairman of the ICCC Teachers Committee for his input to this concept.)

29

Good building

A wise builder will look to be building on rock, as we saw from the parable in Matthew 7. The underlayer upon which the foundation is to be built is rock. The foundation will support the actual building and so needs to be sound.

From the diagram on the previous page you will note that our motive is like the foundation of the building – even if we are building on rock underneath, still the foundation needs to be strong and bedded on to the rock with the experiences of our faith.

> *'Faith without works is dead.'*   (James 2:26)

Then the underlayer and the foundation will take on the same characteristic – the strong safe characteristic of Jesus as the rock.

Good intentions

Think again about the man, John, to whom reference was made in the introduction. He was a believer – in that sense his life was built on rock, but his motive in starting his business was sand. It appeared good to his thinking, but his thinking was not in line with God's thinking.

I'm afraid, as an accountant, I hear this quite often. Some- one starts a business with the intention of blessing God's kingdom with finance; i.e. the motive or foundation upon which the business is built is money. Oh it seems good, because it's money for God, but actually it's sand.

God does not need our money, for actually He owns everything anyway. What He so wants is a deep relationship with us in which we love Him and receive His love. As we described earlier, our increasing love for Him will lead us more and more to obey His voice. If He tells us to start or run a business to make money and plough the money into His kingdom, that is a different matter, for our motive becomes one of obedience.

It is true to say that out of the overflow of blessing that God does pour into an obedient life, He expects us to be generous and hilarious givers. That is quite different from a motive to make money for God.

Good foundations

A proper motive is the only sound foundation and we are really expected to have one motive – and that is to please God.

Pleasing God is simple – it's obediently following His voice. The difficulties arise in hearing something we don't want to hear and in resisting our own ideas, which somehow always seem so 'wise and wonderful'.

Each one of us will give an account of himself to God (Romans 14:12) and therefore we would do well to have as our ambition in this life, to please Him.

> *'Therefore also we have as our ambition, whether at home or absent, to be pleasing to Him.'*   (2 Corinthians 5:9)

Unless the Lord builds the house

> *'Unless the Lord build the house, they labour in vain who build it.'*   (Psalm 127:1)

If only we really understood that God wants to use us to share in what He is doing and does not want our schemes and good ideas, we would avoid so many disasters.

Jesus said that He only did what He saw and heard His Father doing (from John 5:19 and 30), and the Scripture tells us that we are like Him and to be like Him (from 1 John 4:17). Therefore we should be doing what we see the Father doing. The result of joining Him in what He is doing is to please Him.

This is achieved in the same way that Jesus achieved it – by doing what we see and hear the Father doing. A huge amount of useless activity would cease and a great more would be achieved if every Christian walked this way. But the facts are not so straightforward: we learn a little, fall, repent and start over again. Sometimes it seems that we have changed little, still falling into the trap of doing, rather than waiting for instructions.

It is so good to realise that there is no condemnation for our failures and that God encourages us to go on, listening and learning to hear, seeing and learning to see what He is doing. Then we will, in due course, be able to look back and see that we have progressed. Our lives have changed and are changing, we are more in love with Jesus now than we were before, and we are more pleasing to God.

My own motives

Yes, my motives had to change. My personal job enjoyment was no longer a valid motive, nor was my desire to run a profitable business.

During the period of unemployment I was learning things I should have learnt much earlier in my Christian life. Indeed I probably would have saved myself from many troubles if I had learnt to love God, really love Him, earlier on. But then it often seems we have to learn the hard way. I know that I am not alone in this – sadly it is a common experience.

Where would God lead me?

I applied for many jobs during the six months I spent out of work. At first I thought that getting a new job would be easy; after all I was qualified, experienced and had a good track record.

My heavenly Father knows best and He had plans for me. However, as it turned out, those plans would take time to develop.

I was extremely pleased after six months to be offered a job with a life insurance company selling life insurance. Believe me, after unemployment, you can be willing to try anything.

God was in it – not that I'd heard His voice telling me to go this way – not yet. But now I was asking to be led, was willing to submit to His way, was praying regularly and was beginning to enjoy a closer relationship with Him.

Unknowingly I was going into His training school.

But where would God lead me...?

Chapter 4

In the Wilderness

Over a period of time a new concept became clear to me: if God had a particular plan for my life and if His plans for me were for my welfare, then there was a 'promised land' for me to enter.

Entering this 'land' however, was not straightforward – it involved being led into a new way of thinking and acting.

Once I believed that there was a promised land to enter, the act of trusting God as provider became crucial. This was a process which would prove difficult to learn, but fortunately, in the Scripture I found a blue print. Not that the circumstances were the same, but the principles came through the scriptural story and were directly relevant to my situation.

The blue print

In Genesis it tells us that in the beginning God had made everything well, and He proclaimed that His creation was good. He warned man that disobedience would lead to death and then, as a result of man's disobedience, He cursed the ground and subjected man to toil.

> *'By the sweat of your face you shall eat bread.'*
> (Genesis 3:19)

Man went from bad to worse and God decided to wipe out His creation, except that Noah found favour, obeyed God's instruction to build the ark, and was saved through the flood with his family.

God then promised not to flood the earth again and that seed time and harvest would continue.

Abraham also heard God make him amazing promises, if he would take God at His word. He did and was greatly blessed.

You could say that Genesis is a story of God's desire to bless His creation and man's response. That response was mainly in failure, but with just enough obedience to establish the human race and the line from which the Saviour would come.

Blessing in the work place

With Moses, God introduced what we call the Law. This Law had promises of great blessing.

My office is a converted barn so we have had along one wall a statement from the Law, in the form of a huge banner, *'The Lord will command the blessing on you in your barn'* (Deuteronomy 28:8) to continually remind us of His desire to bless.

That chapter of Deuteronomy has great promises of blessing, such as that the blessing shall come upon you and overtake you. However, it also has equally great warnings of cursing for disobedience.

The point of the Law

The purpose of the Law was not that we should be able to fulfil it (for God knows the heart of man) rather that the Law should be a teacher. It teaches us of the need of a Saviour and a need of God's grace, in fact, leading us to Christ.

> *'Therefore the Law has become our tutor to lead us to Christ, that we may be justified by faith.'*
>
> (Galatians 3:24)

The curse removed

For the one who has been born again and thus believes, Jesus has removed the curse of the Law:

> *'Christ redeemed us from the curse of the law, having become a curse for us.'*   (Galatians 3:13)

The curse having been removed actually only leaves the promise of blessing, to be appropriated by trust and faith.

'In Him we live and move and have our being'

This bold statement of Scripture is found in Acts 17:28. This statement is true, God is everywhere, so all we do is in Him. However, not all we do is **of** Him. In fact, I would have to be honest and say that as far as my working life was concerned, very little, if anything, could be said to be **of** God once I had stepped out of accountancy into general management.

Into the world's work systems

Outside of the particular purpose of God, I had, without realising it, entered the world work system. In my study I can now identify two world work systems. There may well be others:

The Egypt system

The Jews were in Egypt and subjected to a hard labour which got progressively harder; the story is in Exodus chapter 5. They were the brickmakers to Pharaoh and were given both a quota to produce and the materials necessary. A hard enough task, which increased in difficulty when they were told to get their own materials and still required to produce the same quota.

Many, many people are stuck in 'Egypt-like' work systems today – all hard labour and not getting any easier!

The Babylon system

The use of 'spiritual' forces of darkness for business purposes. Paul met up with this system in Ephesus. A man named Demetrius had 'a nice little earner' making idols of Artemis. As the gospel impacted the area the demand for idols was reduced and a riot broke out (see Acts 19).

The Babylon system is strongly anti-Christian. In Revelation 17:6 we see Babylon depicted as a woman:

> *'and I saw the woman drunk with the blood of the saints and with the blood of the witnesses of Jesus.'*

God will deal with this system finally; its downfall is seen in Revelation 18:15.

In the meantime the system is spreading greatly. The teaching of the 'New Age', that 'we are all gods', is a part of the Babylon system. Freemasonry, fortune telling, blessing by spiritists, guidance by stars and spirit guides, these and all ways that tap into 'spiritual' wisdom other than that provided by Jesus are Babylonian.

Are you working in one of these systems?

I was. It wasn't apparent at the time, for my conception of running the plastics factory was one of enjoyment. However, when I look back it involved long hours including some weekend time. Although my salary was 'excellent' the truth is that my family suffered. I wasn't there to have input into the lives of our three growing children and our material well-being did not compensate them or my wife.

Not only that, I was slipping away from my relationship with Jesus. I was born again but not deeply in love with the Lord and the draw of the business world drew me away. My life was becoming less and less Christian and more and more worldly and sinful.

What about you?

So is there another way?

Jacob was working as a shepherd for Laban for the hand of his second daughter, Rachel. At the wedding feast he is tricked and finds himself married to the elder daughter, Leah. Laban allows him Rachel also, but only when he agrees to another seven years of work.

Fourteen years of work, two wives and no assets. He seeks something from Laban. The story is found in Genesis chapters 30 and 31.

In short, a division of the flock was agreed. The striped, spotted, speckled and black are to be Jacob's, the rest Laban's.

God introduces a new work system. In a dream Jacob saw how spotted, speckled and black sheep were produced as the flock mated. To identify with the dream he placed reeds, with stripes created by peeling away some of the reed, beside the water troughs.

The result was that Jacob's flock increased vastly. So much so that he became *'exceedingly prosperous'*. God had blessed him greatly through personal revelation.

Another work scene

The builders were cutting trees to build a bigger house. One chap's axe-head flew off as he chopped down a tree and it fell into the river and sank. Regrettably, the axe was not his, but was borrowed. The builder was with the prophet Elisha at the time and he called to him for help. Well, Elisha made the axe-head float. All natural logic is defied by this account, yet it came to pass. God sovereignly intervened (2 Kings 6:1–7).

Supernatural intervention

Yes, God will intervene. Two or three years ago I was advising a small plc (public limited company) on a regular basis, producing cash flows, budgets and generally overseeing their accounts function. A significant problem arose due to a big drop in business as the country started to go into recession.

The rolling cash forecast showed that the company was going to be £300,000 short of its requirements in a few months' time. The company had already borrowed the most their bankers would lend and there was no possible source of additional funding.

Explaining the position to the two major shareholders, who also ran the business, I found myself saying to them that I would pray and ask God to send £300,000. Although the two wouldn't say they had faith to believe or that they understood a relationship with God in the way we are talking about, nevertheless they were pleased with my offer.

The Lord we serve is able

Within a couple of weeks a (new) customer insisted on paying in advance for a job my client was going to do for them. So in February, for a job to be done in August, my client received an advance payment of £225,000. This was the first time my client had ever received a payment such as this in advance. This did not accord with their business mind-set, God had responded to prayer.

Then the following week the client received another £75,000, being an immediate payment of 50% for another new job for another new client – this job starting straight away.

The gap was filled. The company survived what would otherwise have most probably been liquidation, and continues to trade profitably as this is written.

Learning from the past

Paul states in 1 Corinthians 10:11 that,

> '*Now these things happened to them* (the Jews in the wilderness and going into the promised land) *as an example, and they were written for our instruction.*'

So we can expect to learn valuable lessons from the story.

The promise

God promised that the land He was leading them to *'flowed with milk and honey'*. A prosperous land, full of good things was to be their inheritance.

All that was required was obedience and trust.

Leaving the old way

The Israelites had to leave Egypt, although Pharaoh did all he could to prevent them from doing so. The parting took place, but Pharaoh sent his army after them. A miracle was essential or the whole story would have ended there. Israel faced the Red Sea ahead of them and the Egyptian army behind them. Unless God intervened they would be lost. What would be the outcome?

God did intervene. The sea was parted; Israel crossed over; the Egyptian army followed and was wiped out as the sea closed in on top of them. A miracle had taken place; the Israelites had been delivered from certain death.

The 'cutting off' from the old life was completed, but, as we shall see, the old life had not been forgotten by the Israelites and this was to lead to continual trouble.

Into the wilderness

One often hears of Christians living through a 'wilderness' experience. The Israelites were to learn lessons in their wilderness experience. Miraculous provision of health, of food, of water and of victory over enemies, even their clothing did not wear out (Deuteronomy 8:4).

They were also going to experience problems:

After only three days they came to Marah and the water was 'undrinkable' (Exodus 16:33 ff.). The people grumbled, Moses called on God and the waters were healed. The people are told to heed and obey God's voice rather than concern themselves with their circumstances.

A little later they are grumbling again, this time over the lack of bread and meat. God sends manna and quail and simple instructions about collecting the manna. The people do not follow God's instructions and He is angry for they are still not trusting Him.

A little later and again no water. The people now 'contend' with Moses, who, on God's instruction, strikes the rock and out flows water.

Then they face Amalek in battle and win, as Aaron and Hur hold up the arms of Moses.

God was wanting a people who would listen

'Now then, if you will indeed obey My voice and keep My covenant, then you shall be My own possession among all the peoples, for all the earth is Mine.'

(Exodus 19:9)

But the people were not interested in hearing God's voice for they were fearful instead of trusting. In Exodus 19:15–25 we read that, the people drew near to the mountain to hear God, but the people trembled and stood at a distance. It's then reported in chapter 20:19 that the people insisted Moses should hear God's voice on their behalf, bringing them messages. They did not want to, and would not, listen to God for themselves.

Experience without benefit

Their experiences should have told them that God was able and willing to meet their every need, that He was on their side, or rather that He wanted them on His side in a place of safety.

But instead, the miraculous provision and deliverence did not have that effect. They grumbled and looked back to Egypt (Numbers chapter 11). It seems incredible that they could look back to the bondage of Egypt and see it as preferable to going into God's promised land; but that is the nature of things when one refuses to hear God's voice and follow; bondage and slavery appear preferable to the 'risk' of trusting God.

Opportunity

When they were on the very edge of the promised land they decided to send in spies to see what the land was like.

> *'We went into the land where you sent us, and it certainly does flow with milk and honey.'*   (Numbers 13:27)

A glowing report and evidence, for they brought with them some of the fruit of the land: one cluster of grapes required two men to carry it slung on a pole between them! (Numbers 13:23).

Two of the twelve spies were confident.

> *'We should by all means go in and take possession of it.'*
> (Numbers 13:30)

But ten spies were overcome by what they saw and brought a bad report.

> *'The inhabitants are too strong for us.'*
> (Numbers 13:31)

Without God their statement was probably true; but God was with them and He had already demonstrated His ability time and again to meet their every need. Thus they had a total lack of trust in He who is trustworthy, that caused them to fail to move according to God's plan for them. (In fact, had they known it, the existing inhabitants were terrified of them; see Joshua 2:9.)

Trust or fear?

This is so like us. We are all faced with various situations and trials. How do we react? Will we ignore God or will we trust in His loving care and ability?

God would not permit that whole generation of Israelites to enter the land, except for the two who brought the good report. For us it is different for we live in the age of grace. There is always another chance if we repent, turning away from our old ways and starting again.

Out of work

My period of unemployment lasted six months, and for the sake of my story, I am looking on that as being likened to being in the wilderness; it certainly felt like it!

I felt disorientated. Day to day there was no office to go to, unless one counts the unemployment office! Each day I would search the papers for relevant job offers and write to any likely possibilities. Occasionally I had the opportunity to attend an interview.

It was not at all like full-time employment. But there were some good things which came out of this period of time. I got to know my family far better than before. A particular blessing was being able to decorate the house from top to bottom. We had moved to the new house a month before I lost my job. The previous occupier had been an elderly lady who only used a couple of rooms and consequently the house was in a poor state.

New skills were necessary: my DIY improved greatly (but then it had more or less constant practice for six months). As the house in on the large side, decoration and repairs filled a lot of my spare time.

However, after six months of unemployment I was now to start a new job.

Chapter 5

Entering the Promised Land

I was to work from the Brighton office of a 'direct sell' life insurance company. Between my interview and the day I started, a gap of a few days, the branch manager was sacked leaving the branch with a temporary fill in. So on the day I started, the company's assistant general manager travelled down from the Midlands and I was to meet him.

It didn't go well: in his opinion there was no chance of my succeeding as a life insurance salesman. In many ways he was right, except that I had started to trust God. So I told him, 'God will provide, you wait and see.' After all, God had spoken to me, 'do not worry about money.'

This remark didn't go down at all well. However, as the company had by then already agreed to take me on, they honoured their commitment. So long as I was producing business they would pay commission in advance of its due date. They would pay a salary for the first month, during which time I was trained in their products, and after that all my income was to come from the commission on sales I made.

What is a Chartered Accountant and experienced Managing Director doing selling life insurance? Although I applied for many jobs in both accountancy and general management, and, although I did obtain a number of interviews, there were no job offers. I just couldn't get any other job.

No two people are treated exactly the same way by our Father. Chris and Charles share how the Lord led them into new business ventures in their testimonies at the end of the book.

The Israelites enter the land

Taking up our Scripture story again, the Israelites did not enter the land at the first opportunity and an entire generation had to die (bar the two faithful ones) and a new generation arise in the wilderness, before the opportunity to enter the promised land was again granted by God.

A new leader

God appointed Joshua to take over from Moses and lead the people into the land.

He had some strong advice for Joshua: *'Be strong and courageous.'* Six times Joshua receives this message. One often hears preachers say, 'if something is repeated in the Scripture two or three times it is important and we should take note.' Here, the message is repeated five times. We will take a closer look at this in a later chapter.

The other strong advice was this:

> *'This book of the law shall not depart from your mouth, but you shall meditate on it day and night, so that you may be careful to do all that is written in it, **for then you will make your way prosperous, and then you will have success.'*** (Joshua 1:8)

Entering the land

When the children of Israel crossed the Jordan river to enter the land it was harvest time. Excellent timing, except that the river is in flood at harvest time. Having crossed into what was enemy territory, the whole army was disabled, as God ordered that all the men be circumcised. Great military strategy, one might think! God, however, says,

> *'My thoughts are not your thoughts, neither are your ways My ways.'* (Isaiah 55:8)

God was not looking for great military strategy or, indeed, anything from Joshua other than obedience to do wholeheartedly that which God spoke to him.

The children of Israel come against their first major obstacle – a walled city called Jericho. However, before they reach Jericho, Joshua has a unique meeting. In his path stands a man with a drawn sword. *'Are you for us or for our enemies?'* Joshua asks. *'Neither,* he replied, *'but as commander of the army of the Lord I have now come'* (Joshua 5:13–15).

Joshua is awe-struck. Up to this point he thought of himself as the commander of the Lord's armies, but now he was meeting the Lord Himself. There is great comfort for us in this picture. Often we think we are on our own, fighting life's battles. Actually, as long as our lives are in fellowship and obedience with God, we too can see the Commander of the Lord's armies ready to fight on our behalf.

The victory was not going to depend upon Joshua and the army, it was going to depend upon the provision of God. That does not mean that the Israelites would not fight, but that they could only win if God gave them the victory. We need to understand the same truth for ourselves.

I was soon to learn the same lesson. It took me a little while to be disabled. In the first couple of months I sold a few policies, mainly to acquaintances. That soon dried up and I began the telephone approach, asking people selected from the telephone directory for an interview.

It was hateful. One day I telephoned a fellow accountant to try to get an interview with him, to sell him life insurance. I was an hour too late – he had died one hour before my call. A distressed young female answered my call. It was not a pleasant experience for her or for me and I said to the Lord 'I can't do this. If you want me in this business you are going to have to provide the sales.' I was 'circumcised' – a painful but necessary experience.

Jericho

The Israelites came to Jericho, a walled city and a formidable obstacle. Joshua received God's battle plan. They were to walk around the city once and to repeat this for six days. On the seventh day they were to walk round the city seven times and then, when God gave the word, Joshua was to have the priests blow the trumpets and the people shout.

Unusual military planning! Not at all what one might expect. But the instructions were spoken by Him who is able to do more than we can think or imagine and who is trustworthy. See what happened when the Lord spoke to Charles in a similar way in his testimony.

The victory was assured, but God had built into His instructions a simple obedience test: **'Do not take any spoil.'**

Ai

It is easy to see how their thinking became 'natural' instead of 'supernatural' after the first stunning victory. 'Well, this is an easy battle, we know what we're doing and this is a small place, so we'll only send a few troops.' The result was disaster and defeat. It seems that they were now presuming that God was with them rather than asking Him for more instructions. The defeat resulted in Joshua seeking and calling upon God.

God reveals to Joshua that there is a problem in the camp. The simple obedience test had resulted in failure. One of the Israelites (Achan) had taken spoil from Jericho. In so doing, Achan had directly disobeyed God's instruction. God tells Joshua that under the circumstances of disobedience Israel cannot stand before her enemies. Joshua and the Israelites repent of their sin and deal with the problem by punishing Achan. Then God reveals a battle plan for Ai and the victory is won.

There were a couple of problems here which we should take note of and avoid repeating in our own lives. Firstly, they did not ask God how to overcome Ai until after their failure, i.e. they were tackling Ai in their own wisdom and strength. Secondly, deliberate disobedience puts us out on our own – away from God's help and protection.

We can fall into this trap so easily. We conquer one situation, experience one great victory against the odds, a smaller problem crops up and we just plough straight in without seeking Him. He wants us to seek Him, and rely upon Him, in everything, because He knows the answers and we don't.

Gibeonites (in come the deceivers)

The Israelites had been instructed not to make any covenant with the occupiers of the land (Exodus 23:32). The Gibeonites were afraid of the Israelites and could see that they would be wiped out, so they contrived a deception. 'We've come a great distance,' they said, to the Israelites. 'Make an agreement with us.' In fact, they had travelled less than ten miles.

However, the appearances of the Gibeonites seemed to confirm the story and Joshua and the leaders of the people made an alliance with the Gibeonites (Joshua 9).

How had they fallen into this trap? *'So the men of Israel did not ask for the counsel of the Lord.'* They did not ask God what they should do (Joshua 9:14). They saw the dried up bread and the worn out wine skins and noted the worn out clothing. The evidence suggested a long journey. It was a planned deception and the Israelites fell into the trap.

One might have thought that after the Ai experience they would have been more careful, but, in truth, are we not just as quick to rely on our own thoughts and ideas and not to consult God?

After my circumcision

Well, I stopped trying to obtain sales opportunities by telephone contact. A number of people approached me for various insurance-related advice. (This is virtually unknown in the direct sell end of the life insurance buisness.) For a few months I was keeping pace with my financing plan. That means I was selling enough policies, which would produce future commission, to stay on the company's books and be paid.

After a few more months however I was in trouble. I had slipped behind and the Assistant General Manager made an appointment for two weeks hence to terminate my employment. This was the man to whom I had boldly said, 'God will provide,' on my first day at work.

In these circumstances you need a miracle. First though, to the best of my knowledge, I was submitted to God.

'Father if you want me in this business please provide the sales. If not, that's fine by me but please provide another job.'

I wasn't full of faith for His provision through this particular job, but I was full of faith that He would provide for me one way or another. It is worth saying here that faith comes by hearing God's particular word to you and not by 'pumping up' confidence. I had heard and I believed, therefore I had faith for His provision.

Equally, I had not heard about this job specifically. Therefore I did not have faith about this job specifically.

Since before qualification I had been doing one very small accountancy job in my spare time for a friend who had a small retail business. The job was simply to produce the year end accounts and to deal with the tax inspector. It amounted to only a few hours work each year. However, this business had flourished and was by now making substantial profits.

In the intervening two week period, pending my appointment with the Assistant General Manager, this client asked me to set up for him and his wife a substantial company pension scheme. The commission from the 'sale' was very significant.

In fact, when the Assistant General Manager met me as arranged, instead of terminating my employment, he had to congratulate me on becoming one of the top twenty-five salesmen in the country, and I was awarded the following 'prizes': a brief case, a carriage clock, a watch, a weekend in Torquay and a week in Portugal with my wife.

The usual pattern in the industry was to work one's way up through levels of achievement, receiving an award at each level. I had been taken by the Lord from the bottom to the top in one move.

During my time with the life company a few people started to ask me to act as their accountant and so an accountancy practice was beginning to become established, little by little. Actually, although I was not setting out to do so, I was returning to the point at which I had gone wrong. I was moving back into straightforward accountancy.

But I didn't see the Gibeonite coming.

A man whom I had known, employed twice, and sacked twice whilst running the plastics factory, contacted me. Now I want to say that what resulted was entirely my fault and there is no blame on him.

He telephoned me and asked me to lunch. I was a little surprised and a little unsure but I went along. As we sat in the steak house, he explained that he was now in business and needed some financial advice; help on a regular basis with his accounting. In our talking he said, 'before you say whether you will help me or not I want to tell you that I have become a Christian.'

He did not know of my faith in Jesus at all. I had never mentioned it, and certainly wasn't living it at the factory where we worked together. We had had no contact since well before I left that job.

Tears filled my eyes as I said to him that I was a Christian and we found reconciliation in the Lord.

He was selling plastic coathangers wholesale; that is to clothing manufacturers principally. This was the product that we had produced so successfully and profitably.

After a while we agreed together to start manufacturing hangers as a joint venture between us. It seemed good to me, I had done it before, knew how to do it, and could 'rely' on making a good salary.

I ignored the unease I felt in my heart about the project and I pushed it away. After all, the project was entirely rational. I was not listening to God. I was not asking God in case He said no. I was falling into a trap and returning to Egypt, from where I had been delivered.

Where is our promised land?

'And if you belong to Christ, then you are Abraham's offspring, heirs according to promise.' (Galatians 3:29)

'in order that in Christ Jesus the blessing of Abraham might come to the Gentiles, so that we might receive the promise of the Spirit through faith.' (Galatians 3:14)

Our promised land is a land inherited through faith.

Faith comes by hearing; not by ignoring, and not by presuming.

The road to our promised land is:

> *'seek ye first the kingdom of God and His righteousness and all these things will be added to you.'*

> (Matthew 6:33)

Love conquers all

Although I was now going up a blind alley, I had my feet in two camps. The new venture was to involve me part-time, so I kept up both my insurance selling job and the small accountancy practice which was developing.

Most significantly, I was not leaving my relationship with the Lord – I was seeking Him and loving Him and desiring to be right but I was not owning up to my mistake in not having consulted Him. I was acting contrary to my desire to seek Him first in all things.

Meeting the Holy Spirit

It was during this time that I came to realise that the Holy Spirit was a person and part of the Trinity. Reading John chapter 16 I could not get away from the fact that the Holy Spirit was supposed to have some influence over my life. In fact, He was going to lead me and comfort me, He would glorify Jesus and reveal things to me. It was going to be better than if Jesus Himself was here. This was difficult to understand until I saw it for myself and reasoned out the logic.

If Jesus was here on earth, how much of His time would be allocated to each believer? Well it could only be a very small fraction of one's life span.

If, on the other hand, the Holy Spirit was willing to dwell inside me all the time, then that would be a different matter altogether.

How was this to be? I already knew that the Holy Spirit

had caused me to be born again and indwelt my human spirit – but that didn't make so much change to my day to day character. It didn't enable me to heal or to prophesy or to exercise authority over the enemy.

I first met the concept of the 'baptism' or 'being filled' with the Holy Spirit through books and then through observation at meetings of the Full Gospel Businessman's Fellowship International. I quickly understood the scriptural basis, which could be summed up rather like this: when you are born again the Holy Spirit indwells your human spirit rather like a drop of water being put into a cup. When you ask the Lord to baptise you with the Holy Spirit it's rather like the cup being filled to overflowing.

I don't mean that this is always an overwhelming experience – for some it is, for me there were no feelings involved. However, the result was greater understanding, greater revelation. The need to hear God was recognised and the ability to do so developed. The discernment of the works of the enemy and the authority over those works also developed.

For me to receive was a matter of trust. I understood from Luke 11:13 that God was waiting to give the Holy Spirit to those who asked. So I asked. The experiences followed some time later. At first I had to accept by trust that God had granted me the filling of the Holy Spirit and act accordingly.

For my wife it was quite different – she was walking in the garden one day talking to God about it and immediately started to speak in tongues.

Being filled with the Spirit is an essential to receiving all the blessings that abound in God.

Liquidation

After two years the hanger business was liquidated with large losses. My partner and I had, of course, guaranteed the Bank and we faced a £20,000 liability, secured on our homes. We each agreed to take £10,000 of the loss.

The accountancy and insurance business was prospering. It prospered sufficiently for me to purchase two cars and a small van on hire purchase. To help in the accountancy practice I also had a computer, again purchased on HP. (Computers were very expensive at that time, about £10,000.)

So I was in the unusual position of one business liquidating whilst the other was prospering. However, my spending on hire purchase and our personal consumption were running ahead of our earnings. We were spending in advance and ran up both personal account and business account overdrafts.

Although the immediate financial position had become dire what I did have was confidence...

Chapter 6

Confidence

One of the most wonderful aspects of God's character is that He forgives us and cleanses us from all unrighteousness, when we confess our sins (1 John 1:9).

I was confessing and repenting on two major fronts:

Firstly, that I had gone ahead with the plastics venture without getting clearance from the Lord. I was wrong.

Secondly, that in advance of His provision I had bought cars and computers and run up overdrafts. I had also borrowed money to meet what I perceived as needs. I was wrong.

Having earnestly repented and asked for forgiveness, I was now able to cast all my cares and anxieties on Jesus in obedience to the scripture (Philippians 4:6). I came to the amazing realisation that He has set me free from the problems. They were still there, but now I knew that Jesus was taking care of them I could experience His peace.

Confidence by knowing the character of God

I had come to know that God's plans for me were for good, not for evil, as so clearly put in Jeremiah 29:11:

> *'For I know the plans I have for you, declares the Lord, plans for your welfare and not for calamity to give you a future and a hope.'*

Jesus' intention was clear,

'I have come to give you life more abundantly.'

(John 10:10)

So often we are quick to blame God when something does not work out the way we want or expect or some disaster strikes. We don't pay attention when Jesus says of the devil,

'the thief comes only to steal, to kill, and destroy.'

(John 10:10)

Instead of blaming the culprit we quickly blame God and in so doing cut ourselves off from the very one who can bring deliverence.

Paul states part of God's character like this:

'And we know that God causes all things to work together for good to those who love God, to those who are called according to His purpose.'   (Romans 8:28)

Rather we should see evil for evil and good for good. God is good and cannot be tainted by evil.

'Every good thing bestowed and every perfect gift is from above, coming down from the Father of lights, with whom there is no variation, or shifting shadow.'

(James 1:17)

Tribulation

Jesus said we would experience tribulation in this life; He did not say He was the author of that tribulation, or that it is His perfect will for us. Tribulation is a result of the fall of man, the result of sin, aided and abetted by an active enemy.

Confidence from the promises of God

Having ascertained that God's character is good all the time and His will towards is good, all the time, we can begin to see and receive His promises.

From God's promises hope will develop. Biblical hope is the certainty of a future blessing. Because I know His character, I can believe His promises and be certain of future blessing.

We find many of God's promises declared in Scripture.

> '*All scripture is inspired by God and profitable for teaching, reproof, correction and training in righteousness, that the man of God may be fitted for every purpose, fully equipped for every good work.*'   (2 Timothy 3:16–17)

As a businessman one has an eye for profit and here is Scripture promising something profitable. That sounds good to me. Not only that...

> '*The word of our God stands forever.*'   (Isaiah 40:8)

So, if 'all scripture' was profitable then, it will be profitable now.

Learning to believe the promises

My wife and I went through a learning process to which we were introduced by some typewritten notes circulated in Christian circles some years ago.

The notes were about biblical meditation.

Replacing doubt with belief

The problem was doubt, otherwise known as unbelief. We had spent all our years trained in the world system and had not been educated to expect God to be interventionist.

We had a sort of 'get born again and hang on, when you die you will go to heaven, then everything will be all right', mentality. There was no concept of living in the expectation that God would heal us when we were sick or provide for our needs now.

Everything we knew, in reality, denied the power of God to change things. So we needed a dramatic rethink. There was no instant answer. Little by little we changed as we learnt to meditate on the word of God.

The notes to which I referred would select a scripture: this scripture was then used for several days as a meditation. In practice it worked like this:

Each of us, individually, would spend time alone with the Lord. I used the bedroom – I would lie on the bed in complete comfort, completely still. Then I would repeat the scripture over and over again, out loud, with a gap between each utterance for my mind to dwell on the words.

At first this was very difficult; my mind would be constantly full of other thoughts, often racing with the things I had to do that day. It was impossible to 'meditate' for more than one minute at a time.

However, I persevered and gradually the period of time lengthened and lengthened. Not only was my ability to meditate improving but also the Scripture was becoming real. My beliefs were changing and aligning themselves with God's word. My mind was being renewed.

Some folks accuse me of brain-washing myself. Actually, I thoroughly agree with them – I was washing my brain with the water of the word of God, cleansing out old thought patterns and replacing them with new, inspired, thought patterns from the word of God.

There is no doubt in my mind that meditation in this way has been of fundamental and inestimable value in developing trust in God.

> *'This book of the law shall not depart from your mouth, but you shall meditate on it day and night, so that you may be careful to do according to all that is written in it, for then you will make your way prosperous and then you will have success.'* (Joshua 1:8)

I had a lot of difficulty with the concept of healing. It was clear that Jesus healed in the Bible. At this time we attended a small fellowship where they were always saying 'you were healed, you were healed' as if it was something already accomplished. At the time this was quite a problem for me and I felt a certain amount of resistance to the teaching.

However, I loved the word and wanted to submit to it, so I

started to meditate. *'Surely our diseases He Himself bore and our pains He carried,' 'Jesus healed all who came to Him,' 'by His stripes you were healed.'* There were many scriptures which confirmed that Jesus heals and after meditating on them for many days my view began to change.

Now I can see that, as a matter of legal completion, Jesus has healed me and that when I reach heaven, I will inherit that in all its fullness. I also know that by faith I can enjoy those blessings now.

A certainty

The psalmist who wrote Psalm 119 seems to write in the same vein. Here are just a few examples:

> *'Revive me according to your word.'* (v. 25)
>
> *'Strengthen me according to your word.'* (v. 28)
>
> *'Thy salvation according to your word.'* (v. 41)
>
> *'Be gracious to me according to your word.'* (v. 58)
>
> *'Comfort me according to your word.'* (v. 76)
>
> *'Sustain me according to your word.'* (v. 116)
>
> *'Establish my footsteps in thy word.'* (v. 133)
>
> *'Give me understanding according to your word.'*
> (v. 169)
>
> *'Deliver me according to your word.'* (v. 170)

We find God called by a number of names in the Old Testament. Here are a few examples:

El shaddai	Almighty blesser
Yahweh Tsidkeenu	Our righteousness
Yahweh Nissi	Our banner
Yahweh Jireh	Our provider
Yahweh Rapha	Our healer

With a God like this, who can be against us?

Can I trust God with my life and business?

Well, yes. **Yes** is the answer. This doesn't mean that everything will work out according to **my** plans and **my** desires.
But God is faithful and good will be brought out of everything.

The day came to face my own bank manager

Some time after our ill-judged return to plastics engineering
I was summoned to see the bank manager.

The company had been liquidated and I was repaying the
indebtedness on the company loan, my own business account
overdraft, and my personal account overdraft, at about £800
per month in total.

'Mr Michell, you must repay all you owe **now**.' This man
was rather aggressive and there was no question of continuing with the repayments the previous manager had agreed
with me.

'I'm sorry. I have no money with which to do that,' I said
(a completely true reply).

'Well, you will have to re-mortgage your house.' A nasty
look spread across his face.

By now I was feeling rather affronted; here I was, a son of
God, being somewhat pushed about by this bank manager
who was clearly not a fellow believer!

'You're my bank – you should re-mortgage my house.' My
reply rather took him aback. I was also somewhat surprised
at my own boldness.

'Oh, er, well, you'll have to give me details of your
income.' He reached for a form and began to ask me the
usual questions.

Whilst the plastics factory went bankrupt, God had really
blessed us on two other fronts. My income from the insurance company was running at nearly £20,000 per annum and
the accountancy practice was by now also producing £20,000
per annum.

The net result was that the overdrafts were consolidated
into one mortgage. The bank's initiative merely replaced
overdrafts carrying a charge of base rate plus 3% with a

mortgage carrying base rate. My interest burden was simply reduced by 3%.

A lesson learnt

I learnt one important lesson from this experience ... *'The borrower is slave to the lender'* (Proverbs 22:7).

I resolved never again to borrow for any purpose. No HP, no overdrafts. (I use a credit card solely for convenience, always paying before the due date.)

Good out of bad

One can't say that the time in the plastics factory was good. We had stepped back 'into Egypt' and out of God's will. Nevertheless God was able to bring good out of it.

Firstly, a spiritualist circle was broken up. One of the secretaries, a Christian, was involved in a spiritualist activity. Meeting with a few others she would pray to Jesus to control all events and then summon the dead through a medium. Once my partner and I had pointed out the scriptures which forbid such activity, the circle completely stopped, with repentance both from the secretary and the medium. (Both had been deceived into believing that their activity was acceptable.)

Secondly, at least one staff member was saved. One afternoon a member of my staff asked me if I was doing anything special that evening. I had decided to use the evening for prayer and simply said so. 'Say one for me' she said. 'No, I won't because you are not a child of God.' The words came out so quickly and I walked away wishing I had said something different.

The next day a beaming Melody appeared for work. What had happened? She had become convicted of her God-less condition at home the evening before, as she dwelt on my abrupt answer. She had fallen on her knees and asked Jesus into her life and He had come, had forgiven her and washed her clean.

Thirdly, I learnt an important lesson about borrowing. (I

don't mean to condemn all borrowing by this statement. I had borrowed for consumption and for an unapproved business venture. My advice now is, do not borrow for consumption at all, rather make do. So far as business or house mortgages are concerned, make sure you have heard God saying He approves the course of action before you act.)

Fourthly, through another incident at this time I learnt another lesson.

My wife and I had gone on holiday to Scotland and left my father with the keys to the mini-van and to the midget sports car. Somehow, in moving the vehicles about, he had mixed the keys and we got home to an apologetic father. The key to the mini-van was irrevocably stuck in the midget!

The car was drivable, but not lockable. Because the key was in the ignition, anyone could drive off in the car. Dad took the car to the garage while we were still away and the mechanics were unable to shift the key. A new steering lock was ordered and the existing one would have to be dismantled.

When we arrived home it was still over a week before the parts would arrive at the garage.

My confidence in God was such that I did not believe He wanted me to suffer this simple problem, which brought with it the concern of having the car stolen as it stood outside the factory each day. My confidence in Him also said, 'He can release the key.'

So it was that driving home one day I prayed earnestly for the key to be released from the lock. By the time I got home, a forty-five minute drive, praying and praising all the way I really expected just to remove the key as normal.

I drove into the garage and stopped the engine. Now ... nothing happened, the key was still irrevocably stuck. I went in for dinner a little confused, I was sure the key was just going to come out of the steering lock.

I had been seated for a couple of minutes when our son, then aged thirteen, and knowing nothing about the saga at all, came in. He threw me the key, saying casually, 'Dad you left this in the car.' He had parked his bike next to the car, noticed the key in the lock and just removed it with absolutely no trouble!

The key had resisted the efforts of my father, of the garage mechanics and all my effort and now it had just simply come out.

I learnt that it is good to bring our problems, even trivial ones, to God and very good not to tell Him how to answer.

All this confidence

Confidence was one thing, but it is faith that pleases God and there were more lessons to learn...

Chapter 7

Faith or Presumption?

Life moved on and things were going well. The plastics venture slipped into history whilst both accountancy and insurance continued to prosper.

Now we had one very substantial client for whom we were doing the whole book-keeping function. It was a retail operation which had three big shops. This client represented half of the practice fee income.

The owner of this business received an offer he couldn't refuse for the business and was retained to run the business for a two-year period. The new owners were not keen to have their accounting done 'outside', so they offered me a job.

This was difficult. I didn't want to let down my other clients, and yet to turn down the offer meant I would lose half of my fee income. I prayed. I just could not hear God reply and I didn't know what to do.

Not getting any clear guidance I decided to follow my heart. I was not happy about letting down the other clients, so I refused the new offer, although it was still unquantified at this point, explaining the reasons for my refusal.

The retailers came back with another offer. Would I work four days a week? Again prayer, again no answer, so I followed this procedure: I committed my way to the Lord. 'If this is of You, then yes, if not, then no. Please Lord if it's not right, slam the door shut but if it is right, then open the door.' I bound the enemy. 'Satan I forbid you from affecting this situation one way or the other.' I waited.

The new Group's financial controller was on business in Haywards Heath, so he came to visit me (we live four miles outside the town).

I felt peace about agreeing to work four days a week and would listen to possible terms. The rest of the job negotiation went:

'What salary would you like?'

'£20,000' (1983 – 4-day week).

'That's fine. What car would you like?'

'Ford Granada Estate – top of the range, Ghia etc.'

'That's fine. What holidays would you like?'

'Six weeks.'

'That's fine. Is there any other way we can help you?'

I explained the tax consequences of remaining part self-employed and part employed, if I were to take the job, and the way taxes are levied in arrears on self-employed people. He offered an ex-gratia payment of £12,000 to cover my extra burden, as an inducement.

As soon as I started the job, God spoke to me. 'You won't be in this job very long.' I had wanted to hear His voice but had not done so in the time beforehand, but I had committed my way to Him and now He was speaking.

A time of hard work

Now I entered a time of harder work than I was used to. The practice involved working Fridays and Saturdays, whilst the job took Monday to Thursday. I had more work to do and, it seemed, less time to accomplish it.

I had to learn a new meditation:

'I can do all things through Him who strengthens me.'

(Philippians 4:13)

Enter presumption

One day whilst driving to the main shop in Kingston, I was listening to a tape recording by a rather aggressive lady speaker recounting how she had removed her spectacles and stood in faith for the healing of her short-sightedness. 'If she can do it, I can do it,' was my reaction. I promptly removed my glasses, thanked God for my healing and continued the drive to work.

Arriving home, the general opinion was 'He's crazy,' but our middle daughter was encouraging. 'Great, Dad – where are your glasses?' On recovering them from the car she promptly smashed them to bits and threw them into the bin.

For a year I stood in 'faith' for this healing. Everyone around me thought I was mad. I was!

One night I was driving home from a client late in the evening. It was a little misty and very slippery. It was about midnight. My wife was at home asleep, but abruptly woke up with 'pray for Peter' ringing in her head. She prayed for my safety.

Even if I had been wearing my glasses I would not have managed to avoid the deer which sprang straight out in front of me. Somehow the car slowed down and stopped without skidding and in a straight line. (No ABS in those days.) I survived a little shaken, the car required major rebuilding and the deer disappeared into the blackness.

But it was another incident which caused me to see the folly of my ways.

Driving home one night in foggy conditions, this time with my wife, I couldn't adequately see the white line to keep the car straight. 'Have you been drinking, sir?' asked the police-man after stopping our progress. Well, I hadn't at all. My wife took over the wheel and, at this point, I saw sense.

The next day a visit to the optician and new glasses were on the agenda.

I believed in healing, so what had gone wrong? Should I have persevered longer? (It is quite difficult driving around with very poor eyesight – I couldn't see a car, let alone its number plate, at twenty yards. The angels must have been working overtime as I drove about and even took the family across Europe.)

This seemingly stupid activity actually taught me an unfor-gettable truth:

> *'Faith comes by hearing, and hearing by the word of God.'* (Romans 10:17)

Understanding faith

Faith is probably one of the simplest principles to understand and yet it is hard to grasp. The difficulty arises from our terminology.

So what is faith?

In order to understand 'faith' it is helpful to analyse the way we use the word.

Firstly, we use faith in the sense of 'The Faith', meaning the Christian faith. In this sense it is a summary of what we believe, which in turn is made up of many statements of doctrine.

Secondly, we use faith in the sense of 'trust'. Often we would say 'I have faith in God' when we really mean 'I have trust in God' or better still 'I have hope (certainty of future blessing) in God.'

Thirdly, we have the kind of faith referred to in Romans 10:17. The kind that comes by hearing God speak. My own experience confirms that 'faith' of this type does not rest on anything other than the fact that one has heard the Creator of the universe speak to one personally, and have agreed with, and accepted, that which He has said.

Certainly I can say 'I trust God, I have faith in God' and mean it more as my Christian life deepens and develops. Equally certainly I can look back over many years and recognise that 'faith' in this sense has grown the more I have been committed to love Him. When I've slipped away, so my trust has ebbed and vice versa.

Faith is a foundation

Hebrews 11:1 states:

> *'Faith is the foundation of things hoped for, the substance (or evidence) of things not seen.'*

Simply, this says that, before that which you hope for can materialise, a foundation has to be in place and faith is that foundation. 'Hope' we remember is the certainty of future blessing. Faith will also be the evidence of what you cannot yet see.

How does this come about? By hearing God speak.

So when God said to me 'Peter don't worry about money, I will look after you' a foundation was laid in my life so that the hope of financial security and blessing could be manifested. Over fifteen years of ups and downs, including periods of making mistakes and learning, I can say God has totally honoured His word to me; including providing abundantly and sometimes miraculously.

Into the Greek!

There are two strands of thinking in Christianity today regarding the meaning and usage of the Greek words *'logos'* and *'rhema'*. I am going to explain my understanding in the following paragraphs. However, agreeing with me is not compulsory. If you have a different understanding of these two words, then, where I say *'rhema'* would you think in terms of a word quickened to you personally, and so still be able to receive what I am saying overall.

Logos

This Greek word means 'word' from the perspective of 'the whole revelation'. For example, it is actually one of the names of Jesus – in John chapter 1:

> *'In the beginning was the word* (logos), *and the word* (logos) *was with God, and the word* (logos) *was God.'*
> (v. 1)

> *'And the word* (logos) *became flesh and dwelt among us and we beheld His glory.'* (v. 14)

Colossians 2:9 tells us:

> *'For in Him* (Jesus) *all the fulness of the deity dwells in bodily form.'*

So we can see from this that the statement refers to the whole revelation. In our understanding we mostly wrongly associate it only with the Scripture. It is definitely true that the Scripture is part of the *'logos'* of God, but the Scripture by itself is not the whole *'logos'*.

Graphe

This the Greek word for the Scriptures or the writings. Because in its full sense the *'logos'* is Jesus, it follows that the Scripture is that part of the *'logos'* that is written down. Jesus said the Scriptures spoke of Him.

Rhema

This is a small part, a thought, a sentence. By definition any *'rhema'* will be part of the whole, the *'logos'*. This very close association has led to people thinking that the words are interchangeable. However, let me use a simple illustration:

'I went to the meeting in my car.'

'I went to the meeting in my Granada.'

Both these statements truly record the event. 'Granada' is fully interchangeable with 'car' – for every Granada is a car.

'Car', however, is not fully interchangeable with 'Granada' for not every car is a Granada.

So it is, I believe, that a *'rhema'* is always part of the *'logos'* but *'logos'* only becomes a *'rhema'* when God selects and quickens something specific to one personally.

I believe that *with* this simple *understanding* it becomes clear that the words are not totally interchangeable. Indeed, this is a key element for not falling into the trap of presumption which can come with some 'faith teaching'.

One hears many times, 'stand on the word, stand on the word', and it is easy to imagine God is saying something you want to hear. It is therefore a simple step to take anything out of Scripture, proclaim faith and stand on the word. However, unless the Lord has spoken to us personally it can be just presumption which leads to failure and confusion – just like my experience with my glasses.

So it is that when God speaks something specific to me or you, we can be sure it will come to pass, not because of any power inherent in the *'rhema'* but because He who said it has the power to perform it and is not capable of lying; neither does He trick us in any way.

So *'logos'* refers to the whole revelation and parts of it, whilst *'rhema'* refers to thoughts or sentences out of the *'logos'*, quickened to the hearer or reader for a particular purpose.

There is discussion, even controversy in the Body of Christ over the question of whether *'logos'* and *'rhema'* are interchangeable or different. My understanding is that whilst their meaning is very closely associated, there is a vital difference.

As the *'logos'* is the whole revelation whilst *'rhema'* is a short phrase or saying, it follows that the little piece, the *'rhema'* will always be a part of the whole, the *'logos'*. Whilst the *'logos'* is the foundation of life and to be applied to our lives, we are expected to be like Jesus who did what he saw and heard His Father doing. So it follows that we need to be in constant relationship with the Lord, hearing His voice – otherwise we would become legalistic.

Before moving on I want to stress that both are the inspired Word of God. If we ignore the principles of holiness and obedience laid down in the *'logos'* we will bring trouble upon ourselves – we will be like the foolish builder who built on sand. If we try to work miracles without having heard God's *'rhema'* we will fail and our faith will become confused.

You may not agree with my understanding of *'logos'* and *'rhema'* – it certainly is not compulsory – but from here on please allow that when I mention *'rhema'* I mean a specific word from God.

'Faith' gospel

Often linked with teaching on prosperity or healing there is a strong tendency in some strands of Christianity to say 'stand on the word', and 'if you have enough faith anything can happen'.

Faith for something specific does not come from the

'logos' but from the *'rhema'* or specific word. So faith comes from hearing, and hearing by the *'rhema'* of Christ (Romans 10:17).

One has to understand the following sequence to avoid acting in presumption:

1. God has made wonderful promises in the Scripture, including health and provision so that:

2. We might place our trust in Him and know for a certainty that He will bless us, called 'hope' in the Scripture.

3. He will bring those promises to fulfilment in two different ways:
    (a) As we seek first His kingdom and His righteousness He will add the things we need (Matthew 6:33).
    (b) By faith, i.e. meaning hearing His *'rhema'* word, He will add – often miraculously.

4. When God has spoken, we can stand upon what He has said. In the meantime we can proclaim our trust in the word and in Him.

There is no 'arm-twisting' of God involved, rather the learning of patience and perseverence as we believe and stand firm and wait for the deliverence of God.

We are not expected to 'work up' faith. In fact, we are incapable of doing so, for faith comes from hearing Him speak a *'rhema'* word and not from our effort or confession. It is no good pretending He has spoken and it is no good selecting a small passage from Scripture and saying, 'God has spoken that piece to me now.' We have to learn to hear, and know, when He is speaking, without presuming He has spoken when, in fact, He has not.

No, we are expected to hear His voice. *'My sheep hear my voice'* (John 10:27).

Hearing the voice of God

God speaks in many ways. However, there is one common thread. He may speak:
– through a scripture;
– directly in an audible voice;

– directly in an 'inner' voice;
– through a prophecy;
– through a brother or sister;
– through a teaching or preaching; etc.

We must start from the position that God will not say anything that contradicts Scripture and then look for the witness of the Holy Spirit within.

By this witness you can tell the difference between that which is general and that which is specific. For example, you may read a scripture many times, but then one day it 'leaps' out with a specific meaning. We would say 'God has quickened it to us.'

The quickened word

When God speaks and the Spirit witnesses, we are still left with a choice – to accept or reject.

Faith is released when we receive the word and not if we reject the word.

My experience is that after a *'rhema'* word there will sometimes be a louder voice saying something quite different. For example:

At a Full Gospel Businessmen's Fellowship International (FGBMFI) meeting in Brighton on one occasion, a word was given by the speaker regarding healing in the chest. Straightaway the Spirit witnessed that it was for me. Immediately following that was a louder voice saying 'Don't be so stupid etc., etc.' To my shame I listened to the second voice and did not respond to the first. So I missed the blessing that God wanted to bestow upon me because I did not have faith – I had 'heard' His *'rhema'* word but had rejected it.

> *'Without faith it is impossible to please Him.'*
> (Hebrews 11:6)

> *'With faith as a mustard seed you can speak to mountains and they move.'* (see Matthew 17:20)

Tuning in to *'rhemas'*

God speaks to us all, but often we don't even realise it.
Jesus said in John 5:47,

> *'But if you do not believe Moses' writings, how will you believe My words* ('rhemas')*?'*

Unless we are Bible believers, we run the risk of missing what God is saying to us. The more we doubt the Scriptures the greater the risk of missing out.

In the Old Testament, Joshua was told to meditate on the Law so that his way would become successful. The more we meditate upon the promises of God in the Scripture, the more we will be able to agree with God and hear God when He speaks to us.

Let's look at an example – where Jesus used 'quickened' words to defeat Satan. In Matthew chapter 4 Satan challenges Jesus in the wilderness:

> *'If you are the Son of God, command that these stones become bread.'*　　　　　　　　　　　(Matthew 4:3)

Satan's shot is straight to the point of weakness. Jesus was hungry. However, He was not going to act on what His enemy suggested:

> *'Man shall not live on bread alone, but on every word* (rhema) *that proceeds out of the mouth of God.'*
> 　　　　　　　　　　　　　　　　　　　(Matthew 4:4)

Satan thinks, 'Ah, I know an appropriate word,' and quotes scripture to Jesus,

> *'Jump of this pinnacle because the angels will bear you up.'*　　　　　　　　　　　　　　　(Matthew 4:6)

Jesus replies with another *rhema* word,

'You shall not put the Lord your God to the test.'
(Matthew 4:7)

There is then a challenge and Satan is again rebuffed with a particular word.

The point is this – you cannot live just on the physical realm, and in the spiritual realm you need every *rhema* word that proceeds (present tense – now) from the mouth of God.

Even Satan can quote from Scripture, but it is only that which God is quickening now that is effective in bringing faith that will move mountains. Jesus did not say 'If you have enough faith', He said if you have even minute faith, anything is possible. It is not a question of anything we do – other than hear what God is saying. His word *(rhema)* is a small but very powerful thing – only the size of a mustard seed.

The enemies of faith

In the Gospel of Matthew, Jesus speaks four times of the 'little faith' of the disciples:

Anxiety (Matthew 6:30–21)

Regarding basic provisions, do not be anxious. Anxiety is an enemy of faith. Jesus' promise is that God will provide and His further requirement is that we cast all our cares and anxieties upon Him.

Timidity (Matthew 8:24–26)

Caught in a storm, the disciples were fearful. They had the word of the Son of God that they were going to the other side of the lake (v. 18), so why become timid when the circumstances become adverse?

Doubt (Matthew 14:31)

Peter walks on the water. Again circumstances seem adverse and he doubts. In consequence he begins to sink.

Forgetfulness and lack of understanding (Matthew 16:8–9)

The disciples don't understand Jesus when He makes a reference to 'leaven', wrongly ascribing His statement to the

need of bread. In so doing they forget the miraculous provision of bread for huge crowds on two past but recent
occasions.

By being aware of these illustrations of little faith, we can
seek to avoid making the same mistakes. It is so easy to slip
into the same attitudes in our own lives but these examples
are here in the Scripture so that we are forewarned. Forewarned is forearmed – are you?

The antidote is to be so soaked in the Scripture that the
promises and character of God become more real to us than
mere circumstances.

Chapter 8

Hearing

'Without faith it is impossible to please Him.'
(Hebrews 11:6)

and

> *'so faith comes by hearing and hearing by the word* (rhema) *of Christ.'*   (Romans 10:17)

The question of 'hearing' clearly assumes great importance for a walk of faith pleasing to our Father. So it is
essential to address the question, how does one 'hear' God?

Countless times I have heard my brothers and sisters in
Christ say, 'I don't hear from God,' as if they have some
faculty missing. The Scripture says clearly that, *'My sheep
hear My voice'* (John 10:27).

We can therefore start from the following proposition: it is
expected of every truly born-again believer that he or she has
the capacity to hear God. However, it may well be that any
individual believer has not yet learnt to recognise when God
is speaking.

If we start from a position that says, 'I cannot or do not
hear from God,' or 'God never speaks to me,' we have
closed the door on hearing God speak.

A change of attitude is necessary before we start – a
confession that says, 'I am born again, therefore, regardless
of my present experience, it is my right to hear God speak to
me and I can/will hear Him.' This is a starting place.

Indeed you heard God when you first believed – you may not have recognised it as God speaking, but you only came to belief because you were called.

> *'For whom He foreknew, He also predestined to become conformed to the image of His son, that He might be the first-born among many brethren; and who He predestined, these He also called; and who He called, these He also justified; and whom He justified, these He also glorified.'* (Romans 8:29–30)

Having established the right to hear we must lay a further foundation:

The inability to hear

> *'But if you do not believe his* (Moses') *writings, how will you believe My words* (rhemas).' (John 5:47)

Jesus was speaking to His followers who only had the Old Testament scriptures to go by. We can interpret this to include all the New Testament, without breaching the principle of His statement.

There is a requirement to believe the Scriptures as a prerequisite to believing the things He speaks to us now. This often means we have to change our minds over things we have learnt – for example the Theory of Evolution. God is expecting us to believe Him and in what He says rather than man's theories.

Our daughter Corinne

Corinne is now a fully-trained nurse and has her own personal relationship with Jesus. When she first started her nursing training she was sent home within three months with glandular fever. The normal course of this disease lasts weeks and sometimes months.

Marion (my wife), Corinne and I stood in the kitchen the day she was sent home and prayed as follows:

> Me: 'Father, we know that this sickness it not from you,
> please tell us what we should do about it.'
> The Lord: 'Rebuke the sickness in My name.'
> Me, towards Corinne: 'Glandular fever in the name of
> Jesus I rebuke you and command you to leave my
> daughter.'

By later the same day some of the symptoms had gone,
particularly the swelling and pain in the throat.

The next day, again in the kitchen, we reviewed the position. Corinne was about 50% healed. What next? Were we
to 'stand' in what we had done and expect her to recover
fully or was there something further to do?

> Me: 'Father we have done what you have told us to do,
> do we now just stand in that, or is there anything further
> we should do?'
> The Lord: 'Anoint her with oil in accordance with the
> Scripture.'

(For the sake of those who are particular about the Scripture it speaks in James 5:14 about anointing the sick with oil.
I am not a church elder and Corinne did not go to the same
church as Marion and me. However, the Lord was telling me
to anoint her with oil. I later concluded that it was a question
of authority and that I, as her father, was in a position of
authority, so far as she was concerned.)

Obedient to the Lord's instruction, I anointed her with oil
in the name of the Lord.

Corinne was healed 100%. On telephoning the hospital,
they were insistent that she had been signed off for three
weeks pending the local GP's report and that she could not
return, so she enjoyed an unexpected holiday!

A foundation of belief

How could I address God and say, 'I know this sickness is
not from you?'

The answer is simple, and it comes from understanding
two things:

The Scripture

In Isaiah 53:4 it is clearly stated that *'Surely our sicknesses He Himself bore.'* If Jesus bore our sicknesses, simple logic says that we do not need to bear them ourselves. (For some reason we find it much easier to believe this about sin than we do about sickness.)

However, in case logic is not enough, it is confirmed in Peter's first letter, *'for by His wounds you **were** healed'* (1 Peter 2:24).

It is also apparent that Jesus healed all who came to Him (Matthew 12:15).

This is clearly challenging, because it means giving greater weight to the Scripture than to the circumstances. We find it much easier to believe the circumstances than the Scriptures – but Jesus warned us that unless we believed the Scriptures we would not be able to hear His words (*rhemas*).

His character

The character of God towards us is good. We are children, born of His Spirit, we belong to Him. Even an earthly father, who is by nature evil (Luke 11:13), would not put sickness upon his own child; so how can we accuse God, who is perfect, of doing such a thing?

Yet, the truth is that often we do blame God for sickness, indeed for virtually everything that goes wrong. How wonderfully He puts up with us!

The truth is that God will bring good out of every situation for those that love Him (from Romans 8:28), and that God has good plans for His own:

> *'For I know the plans I have for you declares the Lord, plans for your welfare and not for calamity to give you a future and a hope.'* (Jeremiah 29:11)

What are we going to believe? If we will believe in His goodness and in the Scripture, it lays a foundation for us to hear Him speak; if not, He has warned us that we will not hear His voice.

How do we hear God?

In the example regarding Corinne, already quoted, it was following the thought impressed upon my mind immediately after praying.

Often the enemy will come in such a situation and try to steal the word by snatching it away, saying such things as 'don't be stupid, that won't work.'

There are other ways and I will explain those that are part of my experience, with examples:

The voice of God

In the example with Corinne it was a strong impression in the mind and this is probably the 'norm' so far as I am concerned – by that, I mean I hear God mostly in this way. Very occasionally, the voice has been so strong that it has seemed to be audible – in fact, I would not, on those occasions, have been able to tell you whether it was audible or not.

In both examples it is important that what we hear does not conflict with Scripture. The Scripture stands forever and the enemy masquerades as an angel of light. If in doubt ask God for two or three witnesses.

Through the Scripture (a)

Marion suffered with depression. It is a terrible thing and it used to descend with no warning and for no apparent reason. The depression would then stay around for weeks or months and then just lift. The doctors could only prescribe anti-depressants which helped her through the symptoms to some extent but did not address the problem.

We were on holiday in Cornwall when a depression arrived. At this point I was returning to God from having been back-slidden. By myself in one of the bedrooms, I prayed to God. I couldn't believe He wanted Marion depressed and I was sure He knew the answer, I turned to my Bible which fell open at Jeremiah 23:4,

> 'For thus says the Lord, Behold, I am going to make you a terror to yourself.'

This 'coincided' with having read a book called *Deliver Us From Evil* by Don Basham. The book covered the subject of deliverence from evil spirits.

I was immediately aware what God was saying to me, regarding Marion, that a spirit of terror was the root of the problem.

So, armed with the knowledge of who the enemy was and having read about how to drive out demons I was able to show Marion the answer to her problem. With her agreement I commanded the spirit to go and we both 'saw' it leave. Marion then learnt to stand firm against its attempts to return and she has been free from depression for fifteen years.

Through the Scripture (b)

When we faced bankruptcy, the mortgage, the bank guarantee and other debts at least equalled, if not exceeded the equity in our house. We asked the Lord what we should do and Marion felt that the following scripture was quickened to her as she read it:

> *'If you will indeed stay in this land, then I will build you up and not tear you down, and I will plant you and not uproot you.'* (Jeremiah 42:10)

As the question was, do we stay in the house or do we sell it, the answer was very specific.

The internal witness

When Marion shared the scripture above with me, rather tentatively, there was the immediate internal witness within me. This was God speaking to us.

The internal witness is very important, for not only will the witness say 'yes', to confirm that we are in God's will but He can also be grieved if we move away from His will. The internal witness is the indwelling Holy Spirit, whom God has sent to lead us and guide us, to be our counsellor.

The witness is very difficult to describe except to say that He confirms, and this confirmation brings peace. In fact, I would say that if there is no peace then there is no confirming witness.

The Scripture says that peace should be an arbiter in our hearts.

> *'And let the peace of Christ rule* (or decide) *in your hearts.'* (Colossians 3:15)

It is perhaps easier to describe the feelings associated with grieving the Holy Spirit. An unsettled feeling in the 'gut' is probably the most apt description. It is an uneasy feeling that is not centred in the mind, though undoubtedly there will be questions in the mind. It is important at this point to 'listen' to the feelings of unease and not to rationalise them away – it is very easy to persuade oneself that one's course of action is clearly right.

> *'Every man's way is right in his own eyes.'* (Proverbs 21:2)

and

> *'the way of a fool is right in his own eyes.'* (Proverbs 12:15)

I have noticed that in women this unease often manifests itself as gynaecological problems.

However, we are not looking to our own way but only to walk in the good works God has prepared beforehand for us to walk in, as per Ephesians 2:10.

Prophecy, word of knowledge, word of wisdom

Sometimes God will speak through another believer with one of these manifestations of the Holy Spirit. Each word should be weighed and tested.

Does it agree, or conflict with, Scripture? If it agrees with Scripture, move on to stage two; if not, throw it out straight away.

Do I have the internal witness that this word is correct and that it is meant specifically for me?

Is there another witness? Sometimes we are not sure and we can ask God to confirm His word by two or three witnesses.

We should not be swayed by the person bringing the word, even if he has a wonderful reputation. God wants to speak to us individually and to develop a relationship with us without intermediaries. However, He has different ways of communicating with us and will use them all, so that we are perfected in all things.

Circumstances

Generally speaking, circumstances do not provide sound guidance. The enemy is busy creating circumstances in our lives in order to rob, kill and destroy. He is entitled to do this – see John 10:10.

Sometimes, however, it seems that God just does not answer our prayers. In these situations I have learned the following procedure:

1. Do not take a position but be neutral; i.e be prepared to go in any or either direction and do not 'lean' in a particular direction.
2. Commit the position to the Lord asking Him to rule over the circumstances so that His best will is done.
3. Take authority over the enemy forbidding him from affecting the circumstances in any way whatsoever.
4. Go with the flow – letting peace rule.

Other external sources

Once I had a real problem with Revelation 9:13, where the Scripture talks of an army of 200 million. I tried to visualise such an army – it seemed impossible. So I brought it to the Lord in prayer along the following lines: 'Lord I want to believe your word but this seems impossible, please show me.'

Two days went by and then I read in the *Daily Telegraph*, just a couple of column inches, that China had announced that they could put 200 million men under arms. That is not to say that it is the Chinese army referred to in Revelation – maybe it is, maybe it isn't, but God had confirmed to me that such a thing was possible. My question had been answered.

On another occasion I was going to speak at an FGBMFI dinner and was feeling totally unworthy. Again I was asking God if this was right. Two things happened on the journey: first a scripture reference came to mind. I stopped to look it up – *'You are My witness says the Lord, the servant I have chosen.'* I was still questioning – why me? I passed a very large advertising hoarding which said 'Father knows best' – referring to some product or other. But in my mind came the confirmation that God knew what He was doing and it was right for me to be going to speak at this dinner.

God can use many ways to speak to us and I know that some people have experienced other ways, such as meetings with angels etc. Be open and be careful.

Chapter 9

The Anointed Place

'In the spirit I see that God is going to bless and prosper you.' Nice words to hear. We were in the car travelling the short distance from Lindfield to Ardingly and my American visitor was speaking. I received the words, witnessing that God was speaking.

Why does 'the grass so often seem greener on the other side?' A number of times I have been tempted to think it would be better if I was doing something else, or that I could add another business interest to that to which I have been called.

In discussing this with brothers I found that it was commonplace and a temptation, indeed a snare, which the enemy lays to try to get us out of the anointed place that God has provided.

So what do I mean by the anointed place?

It is very simply the occupation to which God has called or wants to call each individual.

> '*For we are His workmanship, created in Christ Jesus for good works, which God prepared beforehand, that we should walk in them.*' (Ephesians 2:10)

Yes, a particular walk for each one.

It is easy logic to say 'if God has prepared a particular walk for me then that is the place where I will find both His power and blessing and fulfilment.'

It is also the opposite of an evangelical creed which says 'God has equipped me with a good brain and ability – now I must make the best of my life.'

I am not saying that we do not apply our very best skill and endeavour to that which God gives us to do. I am saying that we ought not to walk according to our own desires and efforts saying 'God bless **me** in **my** work.'

Where is the place of anointing for work?

Many Christians, when they are saved think that the only place to be is in 'full-time' service for the Lord.

This is a misnomer. Every believer is in full-time service for the Lord. Secular work is to be done *'as for the Lord, rather than for men'* (Colossians 3:23).

People in secular work have opportunities to shine, stand and speak for Jesus that those in 'full-time' Christian work never have. God does not differentiate; He just wants each of us to walk in His special purpose.

So what does the Scripture say?

> *'Let each man remain in the condition in which he was called* (i.e. at the point of salvation).'
>
> (1 Corinthians 7:20)

In context, the discussion is about marriage, but the principle can be applied in other areas. Clearly if the 'job' one is in when saved is opposed to Scripture, then the whole counsel of Scripture must prevail. By this I mean, for example, that if a burglar is saved he should immediately give up his burglary. However, for more normal occupations the guidance should stand. Stay in the calling in which you were called.

Change direction?

God's best is that we are completely surrendered to His will. He has every right to enforce His will but chooses rather to let us seek and follow Him. He does not want robots, but lovers.

His rights are enshrined in the fact that He bought us with a price, as recorded in 1 Corinthians 6:20. The price was Jesus.

If we submit to Him as owner and therefore boss, it is clear that we should seek and follow His will. He will direct our paths.

> *'And your ears will hear a word behind you, "This is the way, walk in it," whenever you turn to the right or to the left.'*
> (Isaiah 30:21)

We should expect to hear God speak, perhaps in one of the various ways described in the last chapter. Then we can change direction knowing that we remain in His will and in the place of anointing.

The effect of anointing at work

It does not mean that nothing will ever go wrong and that there will never be any problems. Not at all; for the enemy is looking for opportunities to devour. It does mean, however, that we know God is with us at work. Read Katrina's testimony of God's help with various problems later on.

Everything you need will be added to you. That's the promise of Matthew 6:33:

> *'But seek first His kingdom and His righteousness; and all these things shall be added.'*

This is certainly my testimony in accountancy and financial services. We do not advertise in any way. I do not go seeking business. The normal way of developing a practice is to make contact with the local bank managers, solicitors and other professionals on a, 'you scratch my back and I'll scratch yours,' basis or to join some businessmen's club such as Rotary International. I have done none of these things.

God adds work as and when it is needed. It is true to say

that sometimes I might feel I need work and it appears slow in coming, but I surrender to the fact that God knows best.

My testimony is that God provides. Not only just, but He is good and generous. In fact, Hebrews 11:6 says it nicely:

> *'And without faith it is impossible to please Him, for he who comes to God must believe that He is, and that He is a rewarder of those who seek Him.'*

In fact, the word 'rewarder' should be translated 'payer of wages'. I'm on God's payroll!

He builds the house

In the anointed place God builds. Not only that, unless He builds, we labour in vain. Consider Psalm 127:1:

> *'Unless the Lord builds the house, they labour in vain who build it.'*

It doesn't mean that nothing is built unless God builds it, but it does mean that it's a vain exercise to build without God and it certainly will come to nothing in the end.

Paul, in 1 Corinthians chapter 3, urges us to build with gold, silver and precious stones rather than wood, hay and straw because every man's work will be tested. My reward and your reward will at least to some degree depend on how much of our work stands the test; was it God who ordained it or not?

Paul is requiring the Corinthians to become spiritual (v. 1) and to realise that they are fellow workers with God (v. 9). 'O Lord save me from my own ideas and my own efforts, let me hear and follow Your way.'

The abundance of grace

In the anointed place there is an abundance of grace to help in a time of need.

Simple logic would show that if you know you are in His purposes, you can expect His help and provision. Equally, if you are not in His purposes, you cannot expect His help.

> *'Let us therefore draw near with confidence to the throne of grace, that we may receive mercy and may find grace to help in time of need.'*　　　　　　　　(Hebrews 4:16)

Yes, God will come to our aid. Sometimes quickly, sometimes as we are patient, He will come.

Out of line

As you will have gathered, I have been out of line with God's will and purpose during my life.

Sometimes we know that we are out of line, sometimes it is not so clear; sometimes we use our brain to argue that we are in His will when we are not.

Peace is a wonderful yardstick. No peace? Then question yourself, has God spoken to me and I've ignored or disobeyed Him? Have I gone off into something without asking Him?

James laid out a warning:

> *'Come now, you who say, "Today or tomorrow, we shall go to such and such a city* (or job!)*, and spend a year there and engage in business and make a profit."*
>
> *Yet you do not know what your life will be like tomorrow. You are just a vapour that appears for a little while and then vanishes away.*
>
> *Instead, you ought to say, "If the Lord wills, we shall live and also do this or that."*
>
> *But as it is, you boast in your arrogance; all such boasting is evil.*
>
> *Therefore, to one who knows the right thing to do, and does not do it, to him it is sin.'*　　　　(James 4:13–17)

Repentance

I love Jesus with all my heart and sooner or later the error of being out of line has emerged. I recommend loving Jesus totally, extravagantly, because, as I said earlier, God wants lovers not robots. The more you love Him, the more you express that love and the easier it is to be drawn back into His purposes.

Once you realise, the way back is simple:

'If we confess our sins, He is faithful and righteous to forgive us our sins and to cleanse us from all unrighteousness.'
(1 John 1:9)

Repentance of course means that we are going to change direction. It is no good confessing a sin and then continuing in that sin.

Having decided to be corrected and having repented, then one is back into the liberty of the sons of God. Every effort of the enemy speaking into the mind with unworthiness and condemnation is to be resisted. Forgiven is forgiven and cleansed is cleansed. Sometimes we need to keep reminding ourselves of these truths in order to avoid falling into the condemnation of other believers.

The love relationship

From God's perspective it is all about relationship. God chooses to work through you and me. He doesn't have to do it that way: incredibly, He wants His children to work with Him – to co-operate with Him in bringing about His plans.

The multitude were praising Jesus as He entered the city on a colt and the Pharisees complained. Jesus told them that if the people remained silent the stones would cry out instead! (Luke 19:38–39).

God is Father and Father wants sons, sons who love Him. Being in love with Jesus, being in love with Father and being in love with the Holy Spirit is **the most significant factor of the Christian faith** and the highest purpose of our lives.

I love Him, I know I should love Him more, therefore I frequently ask in prayer,

'Father send the Holy Spirit to fill me with more love for
You for I recognise that I can't even love You without
Your help. Fill me with love.'

I recommend this attitude and this prayer with all my heart.

Chapter 10

Working From Rest:
An Answer to Stress

Perhaps one of the greatest difficulties for us, particularly in business, is that of not relying on our own effort. The whole of the world system shrieks at us with the idea that if we strive and push we will succeed.

The difficulty is heightened by the fact that people do seemingly succeed in this world by their own effort. Consider the case of the rich man from Luke 16:19–31. He suceeded and became rich. However he died and his riches availed for nothing, and we are told that in death he was in torment.

As Christians we are called to a different set of values from those of the world. Part of the conflict for us is answered by understanding the difference between fruitfulness and profit. We will consider fruitfulness in chapter 16.

Like Him

It is worth reviewing the purpose of God's calling us into His kingdom.

According to Ephesians 1:18 we are the inheritance of Jesus and in Hebrews 12:2 it records that He endured the cross for the joy set before Him. This cannot relate to His relationship with the Father, because He had that relationship before the cross.

His joy is a Bride, a redeemed people who love and adore Him.

Our calling to be like Him, *'as He is, so also are we in this world'* (1 John 4:17).

We will never achieve Christ-likeness by our effort, but God has said He will do it in us.

> *'For whom He foreknew, He also predestined to be conformed to the image of His Son, that He might be the first-born among many brethren.'* (Romans 8:29)

Being like Him means doing the Father's works

We know from Jesus' own testimony that He did what He saw and heard the Father doing, indeed that He could do nothing of Himself (John 5:19–20).

So we are called to arrive at this position in life: that we are like Him, doing what we 'see and hear' the Father doing.

There remains a rest for the children of God

Hebrews 4 tells us about the rest that God wants us to enter and gives a warning from the experience of the Israelites who failed to enter the rest through unbelief, when they first came to the borders of Canaan.

The Israelites failed because they did not respond to God's voice with trust, rather they took note of the circumstances – in that case giants and walled cities.

In our case the circumstances are different, but God has not changed. Today He says to you and me, *'Enter My rest.'*

> *'For the one who has entered His rest has himself also rested from His works.'* (v. 10)

Here is a call not to stop working, for God has prepared works for us to walk in, but to stop our works, to stop striving, to stop relying upon our own effort, to see the Lord as our provider and source.

Let us be diligent to enter

Verse 11 goes on to exhort us to be diligent to enter and verse 12 gives us a picture to enhance our understanding:

'The word of God is living and active and sharper than any two-edged sword, piercing as far as the division of soul and spirit, of both joints and marrow, and able to judge the thoughts and intentions of the heart.'

The picture is like this:
God's word is sharp and divides between:

Soul	and	Spirit

Joint	and	Marrow

We are called to be led by the spirit:

'For all who are being led by the Spirit of God, these are sons of God.'   (Romans 8:14)

That means obeying the spirit and not the soul. (Soul means the mind, will and emotions – whilst the spirit of man is that part of him which is made in the image of God and which together with the soul and body, make up the whole man.)

The reason is made clearer in the next couplet.

The joint is that which joins together two bones and is the point in the body which appears to have life. Movement is possible by the working of the joints and the appearance of life is there. However, real life is contained in the blood (Leviticus 17:11).

The three main constituent parts of blood are red corpuscles, white corpuscles and platelets. The red corpuscles bring nutrients to the body, the white corpuscles fight disease and the platelets repair damage. Together these bring us a picture of what the Spirit will do also. These three elements of the blood are manufactured in the marrow and passed into the blood stream through small canals at the back of the joints.

So the marrow is the source of real life. In the couplet, (human) spirit is likened to marrow, the spirit is the source of real life whilst that which comes from the soul is like the joint – its only activity.

The message for us in this is to live in the Spirit, where a constant flow of food is provided together with power to fight disease and repair damage. The activity of the soul can have all the appearance of life, but actually the deeds of the flesh lead only to death; whereas the way of the Spirit is life.

> *'For the mind set on the flesh is death, but the mind set on the Spirit is life and peace, because the mind set on the flesh is hostile toward God; for it does not subject itself to the law of God, for it is not even able to do so and those who are in the flesh cannot please God.'*

> (Romans 8:6–8)

What about our working lives?

Are we 'in the flesh' or are we subject to God? How devastating to be found 'hostile' to God because we've never stopped to consider that He might have a purpose for our lives and a work for us to walk in.

Growth comes from the head

When I understood that each part of my body grew as it obtained its instruction from the pituitary gland in my head, I saw a spiritual truth.

Growth comes from the head (Colossians 2:19). Jesus is the head and I'm a part of the body. Jesus is responsible for growth so far as I'm concerned. In my business life, Jesus is responsible for growth, not me.

I do the work He provides at the highest standard I can; He provides the work. He is responsible for the growth. No longer does the business depend on my effort to make it go – it relies on Him, whilst I obediently follow and diligently complete what is before me. I have ceased from striving.

Do not deal treacherously

In Malachi 2:16 there is a warning we would do well to note:

> *'Take heed to your spirit, that you do not deal treacherously.'*

Listen to the inner voice and peace, and be guided thereby.

Pressure of work

All that we've said so far has been to do with striving which is more or less guaranteed to bring stress. However there are other things which can bring stress, one of which is pressure of work.

I have had periods when it has seemed impossible to handle all the work in front of me. Faith and trust is tested by pressure and I learnt a confession that helped greatly:

> *'I can do all things through Him who strengthens me.'*
> (Philippians 4:13)

Of course there is also the throne of grace to approach for help and mercy in a time of need.

Peter commands us as follows:

> *'Humble yourselves, therefore, under the mighty hand of God, that He may exalt you at the proper time, casting all your anxiety upon Him, because He cares for you.'*
> (1 Peter 5:6–7)

Jesus takes all our cares and anxieties, including business and work problems. After all, Jesus spent many years as a workman Himself and therefore has experienced the same types of problems that we face and He has supreme power to change circumstances.

Difficult meetings

As an accountant in practice, I have faced many difficult meetings – or potentially difficult meetings. I learned to cast my care on Jesus and ask Him for favour with the 'opponent' whether he be tax inspector, bank manager or whoever. Some of my potentially worst meetings have been simple and pleasant affairs as a result.

There was a particularly difficult meeting with a tax inspector. I was present with my client and the meeting was not going our way. The tax inspector was being very precise and difficult. I prayed for a spirit of confusion to come over her. She became confused, closed the file and ushered us out of the door. The matter was closed.

Staying in rest

Apart from anxiety mentioned above, there are other enemies of rest.

Ambition

This is a killer. If you are ambitious, as indeed I was dreadfully ambitious, it is impossible to rest. Ambition drives one to accomplish its aims. We are not free to have our own ambitions, however, because of His ownership of us.

Rather let's be like Paul:

> *'Therefore also we have as our ambition ... to be pleasing to Him.'*   (2 Corinthians 5:9)

(Ambition is perhaps more difficult to spot when it has to do with 'ministry'. It can seem so 'right' to want to be the most popular and successful minister of the gospel. So long as we do what we see the Father doing there is no problem but when we move into 'creating' a ministry by our own efforts then we have moved out of line.)

Good conscience and renewed mind

The conscience is given by God as a warning signal. If our intended action offends our conscience then the action should be cancelled. Beware – the mind will try to reason through the wrong action and must be brought to account.

We will deal with this more thoroughly in chapter 12.

However, for the moment, it is enough to say that the mind is where matters are decided one way or another. The mind must be renewed – that is, into agreement with the direction of the Spirit and the bounds of the Scriptures.

Flesh

Paul is so aware of the 'draw' of the flesh that he says it (the flesh) wars with the spirit and that he (Paul) buffets his body to make it his slave (1 Corinthians 9:25).

Being ruled by the flesh will disqualify us from entering His rest.

In this respect the introduction of certain disciplines is to be recommended. Regular Bible reading, prayer and regular giving, all help towards a disciplined life.

My conclusion

I conclude that to enter His rest first requires a vibrant, living relationship of love with my Saviour; and that the more I love Him the more I will obey Him; and the more I obey Him the more I will find myself in His rest.

Chapter 11

The Battle for the Working Life

'For our struggle is not against flesh and blood, but against the rulers, against the powers, against the world forces of this darkness, against the spiritual forces of wickedness in the heavenly places.' (Ephesians 6:12)

But does this apply to our working lives?

The devil's role

Jesus warned us in John 10:10 that the thief comes only to steal, and to kill and to destroy.

'The devil is going to try to rob you of a part of your business.' I heard the Spirit say this to me regarding part of my business activity.

When I was running the plastics factory, our product line, as I have said, was coathangers. We made millions of them for the garment industry. When I left the business, a customer who had become a friend asked me to help him develop a hanger specifically for the hotel industry – one of those without a hook so that the guests would leave them behind when they checked out.

We had the designs done by a professional design team and I went with him to Spain where we had the injection moulding tool made. In some ways this was a real venture of faith for me – we travelled to Spain in a single engine plane owned by my friend.

The product has been in production now for fourteen years and I have acted as an intermediary, buying at one price and selling at a higher price, thus making a margin of about 13%.

'The enemy is going to rob you of your hanger business.'

When I heard the warning, action was called for. The problem was spiritual and needed a spiritual response. That response was to speak out loudly against the enemy, taking authority and forbidding him from taking the business.

A letter arrived from my client a few days later explaining that he had obtained another quotation 13% cheaper than mine. This was no surprise, I had been warned.

Now one has to understand this man. He would question one hundredth of a penny on the price of the hanger on the one hand, yet on the other he is a loyal friend who stands by his word.

The problem was not natural, although you could say it had the appearance of a natural business situation. The Spirit had said the problem was an attempt by the enemy to steal and the problem had to be dealt with using spiritual weapons.

I wrote back saying that I could not reduce the price and that he was free to go elsewhere, if he so wanted, or, on the other hand, I would be pleased to continue as before. The business continues today because the spiritual power had been broken by my action.

The same experience of suffering

In 1 Peter 5:8–9 the Scripture says that we all experience the same suffering – that of the pressure of an enemy who is prowling round looking for someone to devour.

> '*Be of sober spirit, be on the alert. Your adversary, the devil, prowls about like a roaring lion, seeking someone to devour. But resist him, firm in your faith, knowing that the same experiences of suffering are being accomplished by your brethren who are in the world.*'

Recognition

Unfortunately it is true to say that the vast majority of Christian businessmen are not aware that a significant proportion of their 'problems' result from enemy activity.

The enemy will attack in any of the following areas:
- Relationships – with staff
    - with customers/clients
    - with suppliers
    - with bankers

He will try to cause breakdown of relationship, disunity and obstruction in relationships.
- Diversion of business.
- Diversion or hold up to cash flow.
- Diversion into expansion that is not of the Lord.
- Whispers of failure – can't, impossible etc.
- Cause errors and omissions and ... anything else he can do to damage you and your working life.

This is not to say that every occurence of these things is enemy inspired. We do not see demons at every hand, but neither do we say that the enemy and his minions are non-existent when the Scripture clearly warns us to be alert.

Discernment is needed

It is necessary to ask for discernment about enemy activity and then to take the required action, as led by the Spirit, to defeat the enemy's plot.

Inherent power

We need to backtrack a little and understand that we have the power to defeat the enemy in every situation and to do that we are going to look at the Scriptures.

The church – God's powerhouse

The church was described by Paul as a mystery – something not revealed in history until the Holy Spirit revealed it through him.

This mystery came in two stages – firstly, that the Gentiles were actually included in the promises, being fellow heirs with the Jews. This part of the revelation is found in Ephesians 3:3–6.

Secondly, that this mystery is *'Christ in you, the hope of glory.'* This is revealed in Colossians 1:26–27.

Christ in you

In fact, in Ephesians 1:18 onwards we can pick up Paul's prayer:

> *'I pray that the eyes of your heart may be enlightened, so that you may know what is the hope of His calling, what are the riches of the glory of His inheritance in the saints, and what is the surpassing greatness of His power toward us who believe. These are in accordance with the working of the strength of His might which He brought about in Christ, when He raised Him from the dead, and seated Him at His right hand, in the heavenly places, far above all rule and authority and power and dominion, and every name that is named, not only in this age, but also in the one to come. And He put all things in subjection under His feet, and gave Him as head over all things to the church, which is His body, the fulness of Him who fills all in all.'*

A couple of points from this passage:

1. *'The surpassing greatness of His power towards...'* this means going towards and arriving ... i.e. His power towards us comes and resides in us.
2. Every other name, every power is under His feet – yet this passage says clearly that He is the head and we are His body. As you well know, the feet are on the extreme lower point of the body, not the head. Every other rule and power and name is under His feet, i.e. under our feet as we are the body.

We have power

In Luke 10:19 Jesus told the disciples,

> *'I have given you authority to tread upon serpents and scorpions, and over all the power of the enemy.'*

> *'You shall receive power when the Holy Spirit has come upon you.'* (Acts 1:8)

> *'And with great power the apostles were giving witness to the resurrection of the Lord Jesus, and abundant grace was upon them all.'* (Acts 4:33)

> *'For God has not given us a spirit of timidity, but of power and love and discipline.'* (2 Timothy 1:7)

Living in power/Reigning in life

Part of our destiny as believers is to 'reign in life' by receiving the abundance of grace and the gift of righteousness. The ability is based upon a good understanding of all that has been accomplished for us by Jesus on the cross. The value of a foundation of a full understanding of sin defeated and dealt with and the abundance of goodwill and grace from the Father towards us His children, cannot be overstated.

From a good foundation we can move on to recognise the means by which the power against the enemy is worked out.

There are two specific principles here:

Defeating the enemy by badgering

In Luke 18:1–8 we have the story of the widow who comes to the unrighteous judge demanding her rights.

> *'Now He was telling them a parable to show that at all times they ought to pray* (lit: speak out loud) *and not lose heart,* (lit: turn coward) *saying,*
>   *"There was in a certain city a judge who did not fear God, and did not respect man. And there was a widow in*

that city and she kept coming to him, saying, 'Give me legal protection from my opponent.'

And for a while he was unwilling, but afterward he said to himself,

'Even though I do not fear God nor respect man, yet because this widow bothers me, I will give her legal protection, lest by continually coming she wear me out.'"
(Greek 'hupopiazo' which literally means to beat out, to beat black and blue.)

And the Lord said, "Hear what the unrighteous judge said; now shall not God bring about justice for His elect, who cry to Him day and night, and will He delay long over them?

I tell you that He will bring about justice for them speedily. However, when the Son of Man comes, will He find faith on the earth?"' (...or will all have turned coward ... is implied.)

So who's who?

The unrighteous judge must be Satan. He is stated as not being God and not being man. He is also in a position of power – elsewhere he is said to be the prince of this world. His unrighteousness also specifies him as the enemy or maybe a minion of the enemy.

The widow is the Church. In the sense that Jesus, our husband, is not here on the earth, but rather is seated at the right hand of the Father, to that extent we are widows. It is true to say that through the Holy Spirit we have Him within and that He will never leave nor forsake us, but it is also true that He is not here in the flesh.

The effect of the widow badgering 'Satan' for her rights is that she receives those rights in due course.

It is important to realise here that persistence against the enemy is needed if we are to overcome.

Indeed this is confirmed in 1 Peter 5:8–10:

'Be of sober spirit, be on the alert. Your adversary, the devil, prowls about like a roaring lion, seeking someone to devour. But resist him, firm in your faith, knowing *that the same experiences of suffering are being accomplished by your brethren who are in the world.*

And after you have suffered for a little while, the God of all grace, who called you to His eternal glory in Christ, will Himself perfect, confirm, strengthen and establish you.'

As we resist the enemy by demanding our rights and, of course, praying to God, the power of God will move just as the Scripture promises.

If you have persistent business problems or persistent health problems, badger the enemy. But keep at it – the enemy is unwilling to yield but we have the victory in Christ.

The sword of the spirit

In that great passage in Ephesians 6 we read of the sword of the spirit, which is the word of God.

Let's check our armour first:

Loins girded with truth. This has been described as the belt of truth – that keeps your trousers up! In the context of the day, long robes were worn, which needed to be caught up and tucked into the belt so that the men could move freely and quickly when fighting.

Without a thorough understanding of the truth which is then applied to life, i.e. strapped on, defeat is inevitable.

The breastplate of righteousness is described in 1 Thessalonians 5:8 as faith and love. The breastplate covers the largest part of the body which faces the enemy. Knowing the full forgiveness of God, through the sacrifice of the blood of Jesus, applied on a personal basis to oneself – this is the right which allows us to receive the breastplate of righteousness. I am righteous, not because of anything I have done, but because I have received the gift of righteousness by believing in Jesus.

Feet shod with the gospel of peace. This refers to our walk in life. Are we walking the gospel, the truth? Is our way the way of God? Or are we walking our own way?

Shield of faith. Do we trust God? Faith, as we have seen,

has two aspects: trust and hearing. The shield of faith is the trust aspect. Hold up the shield – proclaim your trust in Jesus.

Helmet of salvation. Worn to protect the head – we will consider this in the next chapter. Its function is to protect the mind, to keep it from enemy penetration.

Now we come to the sword of the spirit. This is often misunderstood and described as an attacking weapon. However, it is not a large sword such as a sabre, it is a short sword or dagger. The weapon is for in-fighting and is a counter-strike weapon.

So what is this dagger that can defeat the enemy? It is described as the word of God. Again we hear misinterpretations with this word being aligned with the Bible. The word here is the *'rhema'*, the specific word God gives in the situation and not the overall word of God.

Other things to do

There are other 'weapons of our warfare' which will be covered in the course of the book. The two described in this chapter are specific to defeating the enemy, whilst such things as prayer and praise have dual or multiple roles.

Be strong in the battle for your working life

It is time for us to wake up and realise that there is a battle going on, to seek discernment, to stand and when we have done everything to stand and keep standing. It's time to stop being tossed to and fro by the enemy and by circumstances. **It is time to stand**.

Talking horse sense to a recalcitrant horse

Dad of course is expected to know all the answers, especially by his young daughters with problems. This day Kerry (daughter age 12) had a problem with her horse. In fact for a couple of weeks it had been in one of its difficult moods. The purpose of having the horse, Topsy, by name, was for Kerry to be able to ride her. The problem was that Topsy could not be caught. No matter how hard one tried, including all sorts of bribery, she was not to be caught.

So Kerry looked to me (the answer to all life's problems!) to catch Topsy and put an end to the problem. However it was not all that simple. Topsy had not been catchable for quite a while. I decided on the only route possible – to ask my Father who knows all the answers.

'Father, what is the matter with Topsy? How can I catch her?' The Lord spoke to me – 'She has a wild spirit.' I had learnt a bit about spirits and dealt with them in humans, but in animals, this was new.

I climbed over the fence and got into the field with Topsy and started to address the wild spirit, commanding it to come out in the name of Jesus. This caused a significant reaction. Topsy started to charge at me time and again. After a few charges (quite a frightening experience) I decided to continue the treatment from the other side of the fence.

I continued to command the wild spirit to depart. After about five minutes Topsy stood still and started to yawn, enormous yawns which went on for a few minutes. All the time I continued my commands until she stopped. She then walked up to me as calm and nice as you could wish. From that point we never again had any problem catching Topsy; she was a changed horse.

I have used this example because it is so graphic. In business there are many things which are recalcitrant and many things through which the enemy can bring disruption. I am not suggesting that one tries to remove spirits left, right and centre. What I am saying is that the Lord knows the answer.

We are slow to ask Him, it is as if we think He can't possibly be interested or maybe we think He couldn't help. In the word He says there is an abundance of grace to help in time of need. He told me what was wrong which gave me the way to correct the problem.

Why not ask, and apply the answers to remove the problems? Sometimes it will mean spiritual warfare like this example; other times it will be different. You have not because you ask not.

Chapter 12

The Battle in the Mind

If one had to emphasise one particular area of spiritual warfare, this would be the one.

If there is one place in which battles are won or lost, this is that area: the mind.

Our thinking – a blessing or a curse

It is true. The thoughts that I allow to dwell in my thinking can and do have a profound effect upon my life. The thoughts will lead to blessing or cursing.

My thoughts can agree with the truth, as revealed in the Scripture and in the Spirit and in the character of God. In so doing they can be an open doorway to the working of God's power in my life.

On the other hand, my thoughts can deny the truth and so effectively thwart the work of Jesus on the cross to a greater or lesser extent.

Basics first

God is interested in my working life. Logic would decree that to be the case. He sent Jesus, an inestimable price to pay for me and you, to redeem us and to bring us into a relationship with Himself as Father, with Jesus as bridegroom and with the Spirit as counsellor. It would then be illogical for God to have no interest in the working life which takes up so much of our time.

God, in each aspect of the Trinity, is a lover of mankind as a primary matter, i.e. God prefers to be a lover than a disciplinarian, though His love insists that He disciplines us when necessary – for our own good.

God loves you and me

It is vital to appreciate and appropriate for ourselves this truth. God loves you and therefore He wants only good for you.

Unfortunately one frequently hears blood-bought believers saying that God has inflicted them with some problem or disease. This is usually done adding, 'God is trying to tell or teach me something.'

It is definitely true that our own actions may bring bad consequences or that circumstances may be against us and that the enemy is against us; but the witness of Scripture is that God is for us:

> '"I know the plans I have for you," declares the Lord, "plans for welfare and not for calamity to give you a future and a hope."' (Jeremiah 29:11)

God brings good out of bad

It is more than God just having good plans for us, He will even bring good out of our mistakes.

> 'And we know that God causes all things to work together for good to those who love God.' (Romans 8:28)

Our thinking needs to align with Scripture:
Jesus said:

> 'The thief comes only to steal, and kill, and destroy: I came that they might have life and might have it abundantly.' (John 10:10)

It is time to stop attributing the bad things that happen to us, to God and realise their true origin – either just natural, or the result of our own actions, or the result of enemy activity.

Bride

The more one dwells upon these truths the more obvious it is that, as Christ's bride, we are in the most treasured position. No normal human husband would inflict his bride with sickness or poverty or oppression. How dare we even conceive that the perfect husband, Jesus Himself, would act in that manner?

Only good comes from God

This then becomes our basic thought pattern – only good comes from God.

> '*Every good thing bestowed and every perfect gift is from above, coming down from the Father of lights, with whom there is no variation, or shifting shadow.*'
>
> (James 1:17)

For emphasis I want to draw your attention to this verse – '*every good thing bestowed and every perfect gift is from above,*' from God, with whom there is **no variation**. God does not send bad things.

So this then is God's will for us – that we should in every way benefit from His hand. What then goes wrong?

Disobedience

The Scripture gives warning that if we will persist in disobeying God, then we will be handed over to our disobedience. In Romans 1 it is clearly stated that God gives men over to their lusts if they do not walk in righteousness.

The Scripture does not say that God is making man sin:

> *'Let no-one say when he is tempted, "I am being tempted by God;" for God cannot be tempted by evil, and He Himself does not tempt anyone. But each one is tempted when he is carried away and enticed by his own lust.'*
>
> (James 1:13–14)

It is our own lust or strong desire that carries us away, if we allow it to do so. The Lord loves us so much however, that He will discipline us as sons, for our own good. If we suffer discipline it will seem hard at the time, but it brings forth its own fruit in our lives. The concept that God will discipline us is quite a different matter than God sending bad things. If we need discipline it is entirely our own fault, and we will need discipline from time to time because we are fallen. We must learn to see that discipline is for our benefit and then it's not so hard to accept.

All the time we live on this earth we will encounter problems. Principally these come from our own flesh and strong desires, from the pressure of the world system and our peers, and from the enemy. God does not send problems; rather He gives the abundance of grace for us to reign over them.

A warning about pride. The Scripture says that God is opposed to the proud. I believe this to be typical of His discipline. God is opposed to all sin and will bring His correction, but particularly pride, for we have nothing except that which He has given us.

Lack of faith

Faith is not something that one can work up to order, for faith comes by hearing the word (*rhema*) of God. But Jesus does warn us that if we don't believe the Scripture, we won't be able to 'hear' the *rhema* word when He does speak to us.

Therefore it is incumbent upon us all to study the Scripture, asking the Holy Spirit to fulfil Jesus' promise by leading us into all truth. It is no good giving a little time to Bible study and expecting to be mighty warriors of faith.

So when proverty, need, sickness strikes, just the times we need to be able to hear God, we are weakened by our own lack of understanding of the Scripture and therefore His character and purposes.

In Luke 18:8 Jesus asks the question,

> *'However, when the Son of Man comes, will He find faith on the earth?'*

What about you? Will He find faith in you?

Persecution

There is no promise in the Scripture that we will be kept free from persecution. Rather Jesus said,

> *'If they persecuted Me, they will persecute you.'*
> (John 15:20)

Count it all joy

James has this to say,

> *'Consider it all joy my brethren, when you encounter various trials, knowing that the testing of your faith produces endurance.'* (James 1:2–3)

This scripture does not say that trials come from God. Trials can come from circumstances and from the enemy (see 1 Peter 5:9 for example).

It is our reaction to trials that is important and that is where the renewing of the mind has such an important part to play.

For example

Even whilst writing this book, a situation occurred which could have thrown me into panic.

A letter arrived from a firm of solicitors demanding payment of nearly £25,000. It was connected with the plastics factory – the one with which I should never have got involved. The venture was a start-up and we had signed the lease of the premises guaranteeing that the Limited company we had formed would honour its commitments to the lease.

The current tenant had defaulted on the rent. Even though about twelve years had gone by, this letter was stating that I was still liable, and was demanding payment within seven days to pay or legal action would be initiated!

This is the point at which one's thinking is vitally important. My thought process went like this:

'Wow! I don't have £25,000, and this doesn't seem right. God has said to me, "Peter don't worry about money – I will look after you." Therefore, if I have to pay this He will provide the means to pay and if I don't have to pay, then this is just an empty threat.'

So my mind was armed for the trial. That is not to say that I didn't have doubts. I did. But when a doubt would raise itself in my mind I was able to 'take hold' of it and compare it to the above, and thus dismiss it.

My solicitor resolved the matter in about three weeks and I was not liable to pay. The point being, that regardless of the outcome, I was able to be strong in my mind and to keep it renewed in the truth and promises of God. By renewing my mind I was not thrown into worry or panic whilst waiting for the outcome.

Taking every thought captive

Renewing the mind is taking captive the thoughts that would try to lead us into sin or into defeat and away from God, His righteousness and His purposes.

Paul put it this way:

> *'For though we walk in the flesh, we do not war according to the flesh, for the weapons of our warfare are not of the flesh, but divinely powerful for the destruction of fortresses. We are destroying speculations and every lofty thing raised up against the knowledge of God, and we are taking every thought captive to the obedience of Christ.'*
>
> (2 Corinthians 10:3–5)

This is the sort of passage that we can easily gloss over with a mental, 'Yes, yes of course we do that,' without actually taking any real notice.

The passage says that we take captive **every** thought to the obedience of Christ. That is, **every** thought is to be subjected to Him.

Subjected to Christ

So what does it mean – subjected to Christ?

Jesus has as one of His personal names *'the word of God'*. This is found in the first chapter of John's gospel where it proclaims that the word was with God, was God, and was made flesh.

In the Greek, 'word' is a translation of *'logos'*. We can see from its association with Jesus that its full meaning is embodied in the whole revelation of God, because Jesus is the manifestation of the fulness of the deity in bodily form (Colossians 2:9).

So our thoughts are to be subjected to the whole truth and those that are found to be lacking, or in opposition, are to be taken captive.

The 'taken captive' is a battle word. It is like taking prisoners of war – in fact, that is the meaning of the Greek. Take your thoughts as prisoners of war!

The Scripture thus confirms, 'the battle is in the mind.'

Before Christ

Before we knew Jesus we walked in the futility of our minds, we are told in Ephesians 4:17. At that time we could know no better, for nothing had been revealed to us of the real truth. Since conversion it is a process of being changed from one degree of glory to another. This process is not forced upon us, so the degree to which we co-operate by agreeing with the truth, will be the degree to which we progress.

Now we have no excuse. Before, we were in darkness, but now we are transferred into light. Do we still dwell in the darkness? If so, whose fault is that?

After Christ

God has accomplished everything for life and godliness:

> *'Seeing that His divine power has granted to us every-thing pertaining to life and godliness, through the true knowledge of Him who called us by His own glory and excellence.'*
> (2 Peter 1:3)

We have no excuse, we should gird our minds for action as Peter exhorts:

> *'Therefore, gird your minds for action, keep sober in spirit, fix your hope completely on the grace to be brought to you at the revelation of Jesus Christ.'*
> (1 Peter 1:13)

The renewing of our mind will transform us and with a transformed mind we will be able to prove the will of God. He also says, *'do not be conformed to this world'* (Paul writing to the Romans in chapter 12).

In our working lives we need to take on board God's word and viewpoint. Pray for your competitors, pay creditors on time or before the due date, do your work as to the Lord, and trade with honesty and integrity.

How to renew the mind

Most of the time it is a simple matter of taking hold of wrong thinking and dismissing it. Sometimes we come under very heavy pressure in the mind and it is hard to conquer our thoughts, so I have listed a few suggestions:
– Pray in tongues – the mind is de-activated.
– Sing praises to God (loudly) – God is enthroned on praise.
– Read Scripture (out loud preferably).
– Use Scripture against the thoughts.
– Pray out loud.

Any of these things will, within a very short time, stop the thought patterns we are trying to break.

Hyper-active mind

Have you got a mind that races all the time? This was one of my problems: my mind would race over things, distracting concentration.

Meditation was a great help in slowing my mind down from hyper-activity and bringing it under control.

By meditating, I mean taking one scripture such as, *'By His stripes you were healed,'* or *'God delights in the prosperity of His servant,'* for example, and repeating it aloud time and time again.

A really comfortable position is a considerable help – quiet and peaceful. Then speak out loud the chosen scripture over and over again. I stick to one scripture for a number of days or sometimes weeks. After a while one's mind becomes totally made up and in agreement with the scripture.

As I have said, you could call the process brain-washing. Indeed that would be a good description, for you are cleaning out the thoughts and ways of the world and replacing them with the truth.

Become strong

In fact, one can deliberately use this process to strengthen weak areas. I used to be very 'weak' on healing. What was worse, the fellowship to which we then belonged seemed to be always referring to *'by His stripes you were healed.'* It just did not seem true.

In fact, I was in grave danger of being found in opposition to the declared scripture. So I meditated day after day on the scripture, both the one above and Isaiah 53:4 – *'surely our sicknesses He Himself bore'* and *'many followed Him and He healed them all'* (Matthew 12:15).

So you can use this technique to strengthen your trust in God. In fact, Joshua was told by God to meditate on the Scripture day and night and that He would make his way both properous and successful (Joshua 1:8).

That was my experience and my trust and faith increased greatly as my mind began to be renewed.

Chapter 13

Defeating the Power of Circumstances

A great multitude amassed against Israel in the day of Jehoshaphat to make war. The circumstances were solidly against Israel. But Israel had been chosen by God and placed in their land by Him.

Jehoshaphat reacted by calling a fast and seeking the Lord, acknowledging His power and remembering His promises.

God said to them, *'You need not fight this battle; station yourselves, stand and see the salvation of the Lord on your behalf.'*

Jehoshaphat called upon the people to place their trust in God and, after consulting the people, they appointed singers and dancers to go before the army. As the singers and dancers sang and praised God, the Lord set an ambush against the enemies who turned against one another and were completely destroyed. When the people of Judah came to the battlefield to look all they could see were dead corpses. (This account is found in 2 Chronicles chapter 20.)

We all face battles

It is no good saying that we do not face battles in our own lives and burying our heads in the sand, for the word of God says that the brethren suffer pressure, from the enemy who is seeking to devour (1 Peter 5:8–9).

We can take much encouragement and instruction from the story above.

Instead of 'drowning' in the circumstances which face us, we can instead put our trust in God and overcome adversities.

If we know we are in the anointed place so far as our lives are concerned we can boldly remember God's promises and expect God to fight on our behalf.

The anointed place

I cannot stress strongly enough that the principles being expounded in this book are actually one whole. It is no good being in a place of disobedience and expecting God to work miracles on your behalf.

Praise – a mighty weapon

Many times I have faced difficult situations, some of my own making and sin, and some of external origin. I have learnt that whatever the circumstances appear to be, praise is always available for me to choose and God is enthroned upon praise.

It is important to repent of any known sin. When my own sin has brought about bad and difficult circumstances, repentance has been a first priority. God won't accept praise offered with dirty hands and an impure heart.

Repentance

We hear a lot about repentance and can get the idea that it is a great long drawn out process only accomplished with great difficulty.

This is not true. The Greek for repent is *'metanoeo'* which means to 'change one's mind and purpose'.

It could be described rather like a boat doing a 180 degree turn. A small boat will accomplish the turn very quickly whilst a huge oil tanker will take much longer to make the correction.

However, the point is that the turn starts when the rudder is moved. A choice has been made and the rudder manipulated to effect the change.

Repentance is like that. We can choose to repent – to turn away from sin. It is also worth remembering that sin is anything we do that is not in God's will, not just the more obvious things. Seemingly good works are sin, unless they come from faith, because the Scripture says that which is not of faith is sin. Our **own** good works are just 'filthy rags' before Him.

For me and you, repentance is a choice to turn away from one course of action and thinking and to adopt another. The new course will be in accordance with righteousness.

God's cleansing is immediate:

> *'If we confess our sins, He is faithful and righteous to forgive us our sins and to cleanse us from all unrighteousness.'* (1 John 1:9)

It is also something common to the saints:

> *'If we say we have not sinned, we make Him a liar, and His word is not in us.'* (1 John 1:10)

(There is a condition attached to God's forgiveness – it's found in Matthew 18, where the gospel tells the story of the two debtors. One owes a huge amount to his master whilst he is in turn owed a very small amount by another servant. The master forgives him his massive debt – but he refuses to forgive his fellow servant the paltry amount owed to him. The result is that the master calls him to account. 'I have forgiven you this massive debt, you should have had the same attitude and forgiven your brother the small debt he owed you. Because of your unforgiveness you are handed over to the tormentors,' The gospel goes on to say that we can expect the same treatment.

Therefore if we want to experience God's forgiveness we

must forgive everybody who owes us a debt or has upset us –
and not just in monetary matters.)

Forgiven is forgiven

God does not seek retribution. The scripture above says we
are cleansed from all unrighteousness. Although sin will
have consequences, through which we may have to walk,
nevertheless we are not to be anxious is any way. The Scripture says we are to cast all our anxieties on Him.

Sometimes we think that as we got ourselves into some
mess or other we will have to get ourselves out of it. This is
not true. It may well be true in the world but in His glorious
Kingdom we can cast our cares on Him.

All too often we cast our cares on Him in the same way
that a fisherman casts his line – only to reel it back in again!

> *'Casting all your anxiety upon Him, because He cares for*
> *you.'* (1 Peter 5:7)

> *'Be anxious for nothing, but in everything by prayer and*
> *supplication with thanksgiving let your requests be made*
> *known to God.'* (Philippians 4:6)

In fact, if we don't, we are falling short – actually sinning
again – because we have failed to apply the word.

Come to praise

So with repentance complete, the choice made, I can come
to the Lord and praise Him. (Once the repentance is done
the Lord may give instruction on something practical to do in
restoration where one's sin has caused loss to a brother.)

However, we should not let anything prevent us from
praising God. There need be no lingering accusation of
unworthiness either from ourselves, or others, or most likely
from the enemy. For there is now no condemnation for those
in Christ Jesus.

Overcome the flesh

Often it will be necessary to push and press into praise. The flesh is at war with the spirit and will hold back, especially if it can use the excuse of circumstances.

However, the Scripture gives us a good example to follow:

Paul and Silas had been stripped of their robes and beaten many times with rods. They were then thrown into prison and their feet fastened into stocks (Acts 16:22 onwards).

What would you or I do in those circumstances?

I know my flesh would not want to praise the Lord – but Paul and Silas prayed and sang praises to God.

Amazing! We are amazed, but should we be?

God is greater than all circumstances

To continue the example above, God moved into the circumstances, there was an earthquake, the doors opened and the chains fell off the prisoners. The jailor is saved with his family and there is great rejoicing and the next day the order comes, 'Release those men.'

Praise, particularly in adverse circumstances, is a powerful force.

Why is praise powerful?

There is nothing else that demonstrates total trust in God like wholehearted praise. Praise, against all the odds, lifts the name of Jesus. He is enthroned upon the praise. The heavenly hosts of wickedness fall back as God's people praise Him wholeheartedly.

Making the choice is the important thing. Entering in and breaking through the resistance of the flesh brings us to a point of victory and peace. Then circumstances have lost their power, because we rest in Him. Either, He will change the circumstances or we will say with Job, *'though He slay me, I will hope in Him'* (Job 13:15).

Rejoice always

> *'Rejoice in the Lord always; again I will say, rejoice!'*
> (Philippians 4:4)

> *'Rejoice always; pray without ceasing; in everything give thanks; for this is God's will for you in Christ Jesus.'*
> (1 Thessalonians 5:16–18)

This is God's will for you – rejoice always.

Rejoice always – it delivers your soul

> *'And though you have not seen Him, you love Him, and though you do not see Him now, but believe in Him, you greatly rejoice with joy inexpressible and full of glory, obtaining as the outcome of your faith the salvation of your souls.'*
> (1 Peter 1:8–9)

'Rejoice' in this verse is *'agalliao'* which means to rejoice greatly, to leap and dance. Peter is exhorting us to rejoice greatly, to leap and dance even in trials –

> *'In this you greatly rejoice, even though now for a little while, if necessary, you have been distressed by various trials.'*
> (1 Peter 1:6)

The point is not to wait to be delivered but to rejoice first and watch the deliverance come.

Salvation of your soul

This is not a reference to salvation in the sense of being born again. You cannot get to heaven without being born again – and that is clearly a matter of rebirth being brought to the human spirit not the soul.

Jesus, in His dialogue with Nicodemus, makes it clear that rebirth is Spirit to spirit (John 3:6).

To understand the difference we need to go back to Eden and to Genesis 2 and 3.

The fall of man

Adam was warned

> *'but from the tree of the knowledge of good and evil you shall not eat, for in the day that you eat from it dying you shall die.'*

Adam ate of the fruit of the tree and lived to be a very old man.

So what did *'dying you shall die'* mean?

God had made man in His image and God is spirit not flesh. So man carried within a flesh body a human spirit. In fact the Scripture says that when God breathed His spirit into the dust of the earth a human soul was formed.

The human being is formed of three parts, body, soul, and spirit. This is confirmed by Paul in 1 Thessalonians 5:23 where he says, *'may your spirit, soul and body be preserved complete.'*

The result of Adam's sin was that his spirit immediately died and his body and soul were doomed to death. That is why Jesus said to Nicodemus, *'You must be born again,'* and *'that which is born of the Spirit is spirit.'* Nicodemus, it is your spirit which needs to be born again, transferred from death to life.

Rejoicing delivers the soul

So back to our scripture in 1 Peter 1:8–9, where Peter says that rejoicing, being the outcome of the expression of our faith, will result in 'the salvation of your soul.'

The word 'salvation' means deliverance from danger. Rejoicing will deliver the soul from danger. The soul is generally regarded as being the mind, the will and the emotions, which could be summed up as the personality.

Most of our battles are won and lost in the mind and praise has an important part to play in the deliverance of our soul.

So the victory over circumstances is in praise and rejoicing.

– Been made redundant? Praise the Lord.
– In a difficult situation? Rejoice greatly.
– Trouble at work? Move into praise.

Your rejoicing, your praise, will deliver your soul. The order will come, 'Release that man.'

Back in 2 Chronicles chapter 20, as the singers and dancers sang and praised God, the Lord set an ambush against the enemies.

Our responsibility – sing, dance, praise.

The Lord's responsibility – to win the battle.

Chapter 14

Prayer in Business

I have always found the word 'prayer' rather dull and unin-
spiring, conjuring up thoughts of the boring, stilted, prayer
meetings of the past. However, my studies in the Bible made
me look at the underlying meaning of the Greek words and I
found a new understanding and a freedom about prayer
which I will share with you.

So that we can look at prayer in good order we will use a
verse in Paul's first letter to Timothy as a guide.

> '*First of all then, I urge that **entreaties** and **prayers**, peti-
> tions and **thanksgivings**, be made on behalf of all men.*'
> (1 Timothy 2:1)

Thanksgivings

The word here does not need any special explanation, for its
meaning is clearly understood. It expresses a gratitude to
God, not only as in this context for one another, but also in
all situations. This does not mean that we need to thank God
for a bad situation but we are called to offer thanksgiving
from within any situation, good or bad, because God is
always worthy of thanks and able to deliver us from trouble.

Thanksgiving is a basis from which to approach our
Father –

> '*Be anxious for nothing, but in everything by prayer and
> supplication with thanksgiving let your requests be made
> known to God.*'
> (Philippians 4:6)

This verse is to be applied to every area of life, to any thing which causes or could cause any form of anxiety; the working life is definitely included. The Lord is both interested and able to intervene on our behalf. Let us therefore come with thanksgiving to Him who is able and willing to meet us when we pray.

> *'And the peace of God, which surpasses all comprehension, shall guard your hearts and minds in Christ Jesus.'*
> (Philippians 4:7)

The result of being able to come and, with thanksgiving, submit our requests to God brings peace. Peace is frequently a missing factor in the working life. Perhaps we don't pray enough regarding that area of our lives. Do we?

Petitions

This is the word that we would consider as intercession – where one stands in the gap for another. A considered request is brought before God usually on behalf of another. Everyone can intercede but for some it is a particular ministry that God gives to them. To an intercessor God will reveal the need, give the burden to pray and reveal how to pray into the particular situation.

As this book is about our personal walk with the Lord at work, it is beyond its scope to examine intercession in any depth.

Prayers

This is a Greek word *'(pros)euchomai'* and is the word most commonly translated 'prayer' in the New Testament.

It means 'to speak out loud' and is found both with and without *'pros'* added to the front. The *'pros'* means 'towards' so in its full meaning it is 'to speak out loud towards'.

The Greek does not have a special word 'pray', it uses every day language. This meaning helped to set me free in prayer. As to pray is to speak out loud to my Father I can do that at any time. In the car, walking the dog, washing the dishes, at home, at work, almost any time I can pray. I do not need a specially consecrated building or any additional artefacts or any special preparation, I can pray anywhere, anytime.

That is not to exclude the need to set aside special time to pray or special places to pray, not at all, but it includes praying anywhere, anytime.

Prayer in this sense is not a whispered thought. I am not dismissing whispered or silent prayers, but in the use of this word it is out loud. Out loud has a power of its own. If you can verbalise a prayer to God it shows an expectancy that God will hear and answer. In fact I suggest that if you cannot pray out loud, then advice, encouragement and prayer from a mature Christian to set you free to do so would be helpful.

Sometimes there are things which come between us and God so that we cannot speak to Him; for example a feeling of unworthiness or guilt. It is not His desire that we should be cut off from Him in this way. Sometimes we just think He won't be interested in our problem or it's too small for Him to bother with or for us to bother Him with. None of this is true. We have been made righteous, our guilt has been washed away. (If we are continuing in sin, then cessation and repentance is necessary.) **God is** interested and wants us to talk to Him even about things which appear to be insignificant.

Entreaties

Meet another Greek word, *'deomai'* meaning 'the expression of need' and to 'make urgent request'.

> *'The urgent request of a righteous man can accomplish much.'* (James 5:16)

How delightful, and gracious of God, that He wants us to express our needs and urgent requests to Him. Father speaks to us through the language breathed by the Spirit when He inspired the Scriptures, saying 'make your urgent request.'

A study of the use of this word would reveal Paul, telling the recipients of his letters, that he and others are making urgent requests on their behalf, and that Paul himself has benefited from the urgent requests others have made for him.

It would also find Peter saying,

> *'The eyes of the Lord are upon the righteous and His ears attend to their urgent requests.'* (1 Peter 3:12)

Jesus also made urgent requests in Hebrews 5:7.

Simon the sorcerer, Anna the prophetess and John the Baptist are all recorded as making urgent requests to God.

Keeping alert

> *'But keep alert at all times making urgent requests, that you may have strength to escape all these things that are about to take place and to stand before the son of man.'*
> (Luke 21:36)

As we saw in earlier chapters, there are enemies aligned against us, as well as problems through natural causes. Make your urgent requests to God, cast your anxiety on Him – it is His will for you to be in peace.

Shamelessness

Jesus told a parable to show that we should be shameless in asking:

> *'And He said to them, suppose one of you shall have a friend, and shall go to him at midnight, and say to him, friend lend me three loaves; for a friend of mine has come to me from a journey and I have nothing to set before him. And from inside he shall answer and may say, do not bother me, the door has already been shut and my children and I are in bed; I cannot get up and give you anything. I tell you, even though he will not get up and*

*give anything because he is his friend, yet because of his
shamelessness he will get up and give him as much as he
needs.'* (Luke 11:5–8)

The parable invites us to ask the Father. It is recorded in
the Scripture in the context of the disciples asking Jesus to
teach them how to pray immediately after the Lord's prayer.
Jesus goes on to say:

*'Ask and it shall be given to you; seek and you shall find;
knock and it shall be opened to you, for everyone who
asks, receives; and he who seeks, finds; and to him who
knocks, it shall be opened.'* (Luke 11:9–10)

In this passage the Greek uses the present imperative
tense which means ask and keep asking, seek and keep
seeking, knock and keep knocking.

As we read on to verses 11 to 13 we find God's promise to
give the Holy Spirit to them that ask. In fact the passage
specifies that you will not receive anything of the enemy, you
will not receive a serpent; you won't receive anything with a
sting in the tail, a scorpion; you will receive that which is
good – a fish, a sign of Christianity; and an egg, nutritious
food.

Ask, seek and knock in the context of the passage would
seem to be linked to the Holy Spirit and a promise that you
will receive.

No blank cheques

There are no 'blank cheques' in prayer. It is not a matter of
asking for anything that comes to mind and God supplying.

According to the weight of Scripture, we should be praying at least as much for one another as for ourselves; and we
can be sure that, if we listen to God, He will show us how to
pray.

So what does one make of a verse which seems to say,
'whatever you ask in My name you shall receive?'

Jesus did what He saw and heard the Father doing. We are

to be like Him in this world, doing what we see and hear the Father doing. Jesus did not presume to pray for healing or for any need just because it was there – He did what He saw and heard the Father doing.

So if we are to pray in the name of Jesus, the same rules must apply.

In fact look at John 15:7:

> *'If you abide in Me and My words abide in you, ask whatever you wish and it will be done for you.'*

This is a qualified promise, i.e. it will only apply if the qualifications are met. The qualifications are twofold:

Firstly, we are to abide in Jesus. A close and continuous relationship.

Secondly, His *rhema* word is to abide in us. His *rhema* word is that which speaks to us specifically, which is then to be mingled with trust.

If we abide in Him and hear His *rhema* then it will come to pass as we agree with Him. One might rephrase it this way: 'Whatever God speaks to us, if we will agree with Him, it will come to pass.'

Prayer at work

I frequently pray about my business in the general sense of asking His presence and blessing with thankfulness for all His benefits. There are often times when specific and sometimes urgent prayer is also needed.

– Pray for your customers (see Charles' testimony).
– Pray for your employers and bosses – pray blessing upon them even if they are unreasonable.
– Pray for your employees or fellows.
– Pray for peace and good relationships.
– Pray for orders.
– Pray for resources of all sorts.
– Pray for your competitors.

> *'In everything with thanksgiving make your request known to God.'*

To conclude

Our Father wants us to speak out loud with our urgent requests to Him, for others, and for ourselves.

The nature of the underlying language makes it clear that God is inviting us to come and speak to Him, to bring Him all our anxieties and cares for He loves us.

Also our Father wants us to hear His voice as we bring our prayers to Him, so that, by virtue of a *'rhema'* word which enables us to pray in His specific will, His power can be released.

Chapter 15

Money

Money has great importance in the daily lives of us all; our system relies on money as its medium of exchange, and to that end it is an important tool.

The Bible, however, describes money as, *'a very little thing'* (Luke 19:17 – in the parable of the money and the ten servants found in verses 11 to 27).

The faithful servant

In Luke chapter 19 we have the account of a nobleman going to a distant country to receive a kingdom and returning. On his return he settles accounts with his servants whom he had left in charge of his property.

Each of the ten servants had received one mina. The first servant has made an additional ten minas. 'Well done, good slave, because you have been faithful in a very little thing, be in authority over ten cities.'

Another comes and returns the master's mina, which he has kept locked away. This man is described as worthless and the mina taken away from him and given to the first.

The point of the story is the servant's faithfulness over the administration of a considerable sum of money (about three years' wages).

Yet this money is described as, *'a very little thing.'*

Who will entrust you with real riches?

> '*He who is faithful in a very little thing, is faithful also in much, and he who is unrighteous in a very little thing, is unrighteous in much. If therefore you have not been faithful in the use of unrighteous mammon, who will entrust the true riches to you?*' (Luke 16:10–11)

A call to faithfulness over money

There is here a clear call to faithfulness over money. In fact such faithfulness is described as a necessity if we are to be given stewardship over true riches.

But what is faithfulness so far as money is concerned?

We will consider money from a number of angles, starting with borrowing.

Borrowing – personal

To give a reasoned view over personal, as opposed to business borrowing, I am going to break the subject into three parts.

1. *Borrowing – house purchase*

Unfortunately it is a fact of life in our society that a mortgage is the usual method of house purchase. Indeed, house prices are so high that, unless one has capital wealth, a mortgage is the only way to secure ownership.

In the recent boom in house prices many were tempted to trade up, taking bigger and bigger mortgages, in order to make a greater capital gain on the inflating house prices.

Similarly, many were tempted to 'cash in' on increasing house values, by taking a further mortgage loan – often for spending on all sorts of consumables.

When the steep rise in house prices was followed by falling prices many people became entangled in financial difficulty. Many people, Christians included are now faced with negative equity as the value of the outstanding mortgage loan exceeds the house value.

So what advice should a Christian adviser give regarding borrowing on mortgage for house purchase?

My opinion is to advise as follows:

Ask and expect clear guidance from God. Do not proceed without clear, confirmed guidance. Do not borrow to speculate on capital gains and do not borrow to spend on consumables.

Consider renting as an alternative. One Christian friend of mine understood from the Lord to sell his house about two years ago. He felt the Lord said to rent a new house rather than buy. However, he went ahead and purchased another house instead of renting. As house prices continued to fall he regrets not obeying the Lord's guidance.

2. Borrowing – transport

For many it is necessary to borrow in order to be able to work at a job. In this case, again listen carefully to our Father, in any event keep borrowing to a minimum. Make do with a second-hand or lower specification vehicle to reduce borrowing to a minimum.

3. Borrowing – consumption

Don't.

Paul says to the Philippians,

> *'I have learned to be content in whatever circumstances I am.'* (Philippians 4:11)

Credit cards should only be used for convenience of record keeping and not for borrowing; i.e. purchases should be paid for in full before the due date.

If you can't 'control' your credit card or your cheque book; if you find the ease and simplicity of use of these items means that you spend beyond your means; then I suggest that they are destroyed and that only cash is used.

Too many people in difficulty

As an accountant I see far too many brothers and sisters in Christ who have borrowed to the top limits of available credit. Commonly this results in strain on marriage and family relationships.

We have been influenced by the world and pressurised into conformity with its patterns. This should not be.

As you will know from earlier testimony, I am speaking from my own experience and my own failure. However, repentance is a choice which is immediately available. Once I had repented and 'vowed' not to borrow again, I found that blessings increased and borrowings were quickly reduced.

Borrowing – business

It is difficult to be dogmatic from Scripture regarding borrowing for business purposes. Again I would say be extremely careful. The number of homes lost to bankers when they were given as security for busines loans is a matter of great sadness and concern.

There is great danger when starting up a businesss – because it is something we want to do. Giving guarantees to the bank is quickly and easily done. Many live to regret this action deeply. If God is leading you to start a business why not ask Him for the finance instead of the bank?

Why not take in an equity partner instead of borrowing?

If God is really leading you to start a business as your walk with Him, then does He need bank finance?

What I am saying here is, be very careful, hear God speak to you, if He says 'borrow from the bank', fine – otherwise you are on your own – good luck!

Love and money

It hardly needs emphasising, but the Scripture says that you cannot love both God and money. We are to love God, because He commands it and because He is abundantly worthy of our love.

We are warned that the love of money is a significant danger:

> *'For the love of money is a root of all sorts of evil and some by longing for it have wandered away from the faith and pierced themselves with many a pang.'*
>
> (1 Timothy 6:10)

This scripture has become true for many who speculated on a rising housing market. They wandered away from the faith in that respect and trusted in their own understanding.

We are also warned that in the last days the love of money, among other things, will become an increasing snare in our walk of faith.

Rather be free from the love of money (1 Timothy 3:3).

The rich

The rich are encouraged to be generous, fixing their eyes and their hope on the Lord and not on their wealth. Those who are rich are in a place of ability to bless many.

Wealth

> *'Do not weary yourselves to gain wealth. Cease from your consideration of it.'* (Proverbs 23:4)

According to Matthew 6:33 God will add the things we need. We should therefore be content with that which He adds to us, giving Him the glory. Seeking after wealth is to love money and that is dangerous, as we have seen.

GIVING AND TITHING

We have already seen that the Lord requires faithfulness from us and so we need to know, what is faithfulness regarding money?

Is tithing a requirement for believers?

A look at the history of tithing

Before considering the history of tithing we must reflect briefly on the nature and purpose of Scripture.

The Old Testament is a book of history – the history of the Jewish people. The Jews had a covenant with God which is fully laid down in the Old Testament. The Old Testament is also a book of prophecy – there are many passages giving insight into future events. It is a book of witness – to the dealings of God with His chosen race. Its also a book of Law – Law for the people under that covenant to live by.

The New Testament is similar in many respects: it contains history – in the actual story of Jesus and the early church; prophecy – in that there are again many passages giving insight into the future; witness – to the dealings of God with the church; law – in the sense that the expectations that God has for His people under the New Covenant are fully explained. (We are not ruled by law because the grace of God has been revealed in Jesus and that grace, as well as fully justifying us, helps us in our weaknesses and continually changes us from one degree of glory to another.)

All born-again believers alive today are members of the Church, the Body of Jesus Christ on earth. So under what regulations does the body of Christ operate?

Dispensations

It is important here to realise that instructions in the Scripture apply to the period of time, or dispensation, to which they refer.

For example, before the flood mankind was vegetarian and afterward meat-eating. (refer to Genesis 1:29 and 9:3). This is not contradictory but 'rules' applicable to different periods of time or dispensations.

Another brief example may be cited:

> *'They will hammer their swords into ploughshares and spears into pruning hooks.'*　　　　(Isaiah 2:4)

> *'Beat your ploughshares into swords and your pruning hooks into spears.'*　　　　(Joel 3:10)

Contradictory? Not at all, because they refer to different periods of time.

When Jesus was asked which of the commandments were the most important, He answered, *'Love the Lord your God with all your heart, soul and mind and love your neighbour as yourself'* (from Matthew 22:37–39).

Instead of emphasising laws He emphasised love. Love is the greatest commandment. God is more interested in our relationship with Him than our activity for Him.

Early Church authority

The apostles and elders and the whole church at Jerusalem laid down these essential requirements for the Gentiles who were coming to faith in Christ:

> *'For it seemed good to the Holy Spirit and to us to lay upon you no greater burden than these essentials: that you abstain from things sacrificed to idols and from blood and from things strangled and from fornication; if you keep yourselves free from such things you will do well.'* (Acts 15:28–29)

Thus, on the authority of the Early Church, apostles and elders, **together with the Holy Spirit**, tithing is not compulsory.

Tithing before the Law

Those who advocate tithing often quote that tithing was in existence before the Law, and therefore, whilst the Law is fulfilled in Jesus, we are not exempt from tithing because it pre-dated the Law.

There are only two examples of pre-Law tithing.

Abraham defeats Chedorlaomer (Genesis 14) and **gave** (not under compulsion) one tenth of the spoil to Melchizedek. There is no suggestion that he 'tithed' (a tithe is a tenth part) at any other time.

Jacob does a deal with God,

> *'If God will be with me ... then I will surely give a tenth to Thee.'* (Genesis 28:20–22)

There is no evidence that such a deal is available today!

What about the Law?

The Law was a tutor leading us to Jesus.

Jesus gave an account of the real meaning of the Law in the Sermon on the Mount, where instead of repeating the letter of the law He stressed the spirit of the law.

For example, no longer, 'do not commit murder,' but now, 'do not be angry with your brother,' No longer, 'do not commit adultery,' but now 'don't look at a woman with lust.'

The Law was not done away with, it was established by God to lead us to recognise the need of a Saviour – to demonstrate to us that we could not keep the Law through our own human effort.

Regarding money, Jesus said in the Sermon on the Mount,

> *'Do not lay up treasure on earth ... but lay up treasure in heaven.'*

> *'The lamp of the body is the eye, if therefore your eye is generous, your whole body will be full of light.'*
> (From Matthew 6)

His emphasis is on giving and generosity.

The Law required three tithes

There were actually three tithes, each of 10% under the Law.

Numbers 18:21 – to support the Levites.

Deuteronomy 14:23 – for the feastdays.

Deuteronomy 26:12 – for the poor (every third year).

Jesus confirmed to those under the Law that they should tithe when He spoke to the Pharisees in Matthew 23:23.

(This passage is sometimes taken out of context and used to promote tithing today – this treatment is inaccurate.)

The Jews robbed God by not paying tithes and offerings and God challenged them with this fact and gave a promise of blessing for tithing and offerings in Malachi 3. But this was to a people under the Law and is not effective today. One often hears this scripture quoted as an incentive to tithe – but it is not operative in this dispensation.

The best way

The Lord owns everything, all that I have is His. The best way is to ask Him at the beginning of every week, 'Father out of that which you have put under my stewardship how much should I give, to whom, and when?'

Let us look again at the nobleman

We considered earlier the nobleman of Luke 19. When he came to bring the servants to account, the servants brought him everything, not just a tenth.

The point is this, we are bought with a price, everything we have is by grace and already belongs to God.

Discipline

> *'On the first day of every week, let each one of you put aside and save, as he may prosper.'*
>
> (1 Corinthians 16:2)

In context, Paul is organising a collection for the hard pressed saints in Jerusalem. He will collect their offering when he comes.

Every week, in accordance with your income, put aside for this collection.

This gives us good guidance on giving.

Every week

At the beginning of every week, i.e. as your first thought –
your firstfruits, not out of what is left over. Seek God first
and give in accordance with His direction.

Generosity and faith

In the New Covenant the rule is this:

> *'Give and it will be given to you, good measure, pressed
> down, shaken together, running over, they will pour into
> your lap. For by your standard of measure it will be
> measured to you in return.'* (Luke 6:38)

There is here a call to generosity, not only for the sake of
the receiver, but in order that God can increase the flow
through you.

Faithfulness

Again, it is faithfulness that is required. Not so-called
faithfulness to a dead law. No, faith comes by hearing and
hearing by the *rhema* word of God (Romans 10:17).

God's purposes

The purposes of God are best known by the Lord, Himself.
He wants to direct our giving so that His purposes are
fulfilled. Often we are told that you must give here or there,
often by church leaders who benefit or are paid out of our
giving, but God requires of us a personal walk with Him in
which we hear His voice.

On one occasion, early in learning this walk with Jesus, I
believed that the Lord said to me, 'give £x to person Y.' I
was uncertain as we were learning, and I asked Marion,
saying 'I think that the Lord is saying we are to give some
money (without telling her how much) to a certain individual

(without telling her who it was). Will you pray and ask God how much and to whom?'

She did not like the challenge but nevertheless sought the Lord. She came back to me with the same amount of money and the same individual.

So we sent off the cheque. The recipient was a full-time Bible teacher who had no income other than gifts. He wrote back, saying, 'Although you would not have known, I have an understanding with God. All the time that my bank balance remains in credit at the end of the month I will remain a full-time Bible teacher. The month that it is over-drawn at the month end is the last month – I will then return to a salaried occupation.'

Our cheque arrived just before the end of the month and took his bank balance just into credit! It was a great joy to be used by God in this manner.

Best practice

So this is the best practice:

At the beginning of every week pray and ask God and do as He directs.

It may or may not include giving to the church or fellow-ship to which you belong that particular week.

It is no good just chopping off a quick 10% (is it net or gross by the way?) and blindly giving it away. There is no faith involved in such action. Without faith it is impossible to please God (Hebrews 11:6).

Faithfulness is not worked out by blind obedience to some supposed creed, but by obedience to the living *rhema* word of God.

Compassion

It is also scriptural to be compassionate and give to those who ask and are in need.

If someone is hungry and asks for food it is no good sending them away with a blessing. No, send them away with food or a full stomach.

The danger of tithing

There is a danger in paying tithes. Under the Law, which has not passed away, there were curses for not obeying. If one now places oneself under the Law again it can invite curses over one's finances.

> *'For as many as are of the works of the Law are under a curse.'*
> (Galatians 3:10)

If we adopt tithing, thinking that God will bless us if we pay Him our tithe, as a matter of duty or law, then quite the opposite can happen and our anticipated blessings can become cursings as we are bound to legalism.

However, it is all a matter of hearing His voice. He might speak to you, you and not some intermediary, saying that He wants you to tithe for a while. If so, you must, of course, obey – and in your obedience you will be greatly blessed. Be open to move on to the best, hearing God every week with specific directions.

Chapter 16

Profit or Fruitfulness?

The world economic situation uses the measure of profit, as related to the capital employed, as its principal business tool for assessing the degree of success or failure of an enterprise. However, the use of a 'monetary' measure is an extremely limited tool. It cannot measure the effects of the business on the standard of life of its suppliers, employees, customers or shareholders.

A business may make substantial profits, yet at the same time cause substantial damage to the environment.

A business may make substantial profits and yet be an awful employer, even exploiting the workforce.

The use of profit or return on capital as a measure is therefore limited.

A businessman may, nevertheless, see his calling in the business realm as one 'to make profits'. In the world system, the methods used are often of secondary importance to the results obtained.

In the Kingdom of God one's calling is not measured by monetary gain – rather we are called to be fruitful, regardless of our occupation.

The call to fruitfulness

'By this is My Father glorified, that you bear much fruit and so prove to be My disciples.'   (John 15:8)

> *'I am the vine, you are the branches; he who abides in Me, and I in him, he bears much fruit; for apart from Me you can do nothing.'*
>
> (John 15:5)

So our 'raison d'etre' is to bear fruit, much fruit.

What is fruit?

In the Christian life fruit will take many forms, as an example:

'What is it about you, you've got something I haven't got.' David's voice spoke out across the room. I was sitting quietly getting on with producing the monthly management accounts. I had been coming once a month to prepare the figures and this was about the third month. When offered the assignment, those few months before, I had wondered and puzzled – did God want me to produce monthly accounts for a company hiring out one-arm bandits and video machines?

Peace within indicated that it was right to continue, so here I was faced with this question!

Without speaking to him or his partner, but just getting on with the job, there had been a silent witness. Yes, the witness was my constant happiness and peace.

'I know Jesus as my personal Saviour, I know I will be with Him in glory in due course.'

Over the next couple of months we talked about Jesus a lot and David's interest was increasing and increasing. He came to a Full Gospel Businessman's Fellowship International dinner where he was born again and delivered.

Fruit had resulted.

Calling

Fruit is the objective. Much fruit is produced when we follow our calling. God has a calling for each one, as we have seen in previous chapters. Following that calling allows the development of fruit.

I have found a certain amount of fruitfulness produced in

my life through the obedience to the call to be an accountant. Though other jobs appear more exciting or more
rewarding, it is only in the place of God's call that the full
fruitfulness can come forth.

In fact, as the flesh is in opposition to the Spirit, there is
bound to be some internal opposition from one's body and
mind. Bringing the body and mind under control, under
obedience to the Spirit is part of becoming more mature.

Through accountancy my family have received abundant
provision – mostly from the normal course of business,
sometimes through clearly miraculous provision.

Others have also benefited, through money, through free
advice, through example and through the working of the
Holy Spirit in ways beyond my understanding.

Over the years about twenty or so people have been saved
as a result of being reached through the accountancy practice
– either as clients or as staff or as business contacts, and
mostly by being taken to FGBMFI meetings where they met
Jesus for themselves. This is one form of fruitfulness.

Just doing a good job for one's clients is also a form of
fruitfulness – less exciting maybe. Nevertheless it demonstrates a diligence and often a love, when one goes beyond
the call of duty.

Demonstrating the nature of Jesus

Fruitfulness is allowing Jesus to demonstrate His nature and
character through us. It is exciting when God uses us to
demonstrate healing and wisdom and knowledge. We should
also expect to be used in these things – because they are part
of the character of Jesus. We should never denigrate the less
exciting fruit.

I remember, very early in my Christian life, there was a
fellow member of the Baptist church we attended; an older
man who radiated the love of Jesus. He didn't have to speak
– in fact I was 'put off' when he spoke about the love of
Jesus, because I was not ready to receive what he said.
However, thirty years later I can still 'see' his face!

Aspects of fruitfulness

Called to bear fruit, enabled to bear fruit and expected to bear fruit, these are the sons of God. We are now going to look as some aspects of fruitfulness:

1. Controlling the tongue

This may seem a strange place to start, but according to James, the tongue can set on fire the course of our lives. In chapter 3, James likens the tongue to a bridle put into the mouth of a horse to control it and to the rudder of a ship. In both cases the 'tools' used are very small yet they control the direction of the horse and the ship, which are huge by comparison.

'Beware,' he says, 'for the tongue is a restless evil and full of deadly poison.' Tough words with a message of great warning. If we really believed and understood that our tongues were full of 'deadly poison' we would be much more careful over what we said.

The trouble is, as usual, that my self-examination reveals a need for much improvement in this area. Are you the same?

Our words can act as a trap, apart from defaming and damaging others, our confession can and will steer the course of our lives.

The mouth speaks out of the fulness of the heart, so our mouths are revealing our innermost being. The 'heart' in Scripture means the combined soul and spirit. The spirit, made in the image of God, born again and indwelt by the Holy Spirit is a well of good clean fresh water. So it is our souls which are the source of the 'bitter' water James describes in verse 11.

We work out the salvation of our souls with fear and trembling and over a period of time, being changed from one degree of glory to another. The tongue will reflect our progress. 'O Father please change me by your Holy Spirit.'

2. Separation

We are not called to be of the world; in it yes, but of it, no. We are in a different economy altogether. Unfortunately the Kingdom economy is more difficult to enter, because it relies on trust in God's word and character, and an active denial of the world's methods.

For the businessman, this is a difficult transition to make, after all, the wordly methods seem to work! Nevertheless, God calls us into a walk of faith completely separated from the systems of the unregenerate world.

This does not mean that my business is exempt from the laws of the land; indeed, I must apply all the rules and be diligent in everything. The fruitfulness of my business life is a different matter. God will bring forth fruit, if I rely upon Him. My reliance is transferred from worldly methods and people and transferred to God, my Father.

In being separate from the world view and methods, I know that God will provide and He may even choose to use what appear to be worldly ways. New clients often come through a recommendation from existing clients, something that, in itself, also happens in the world. However, worldliness often tries to exploit contacts to generate business thus changing the motive from that of serving God to that of serving self.

We are called to be separate from wordly ways. I know it is very easy to slip back. When I was selling life insurance there was the temptation to slip back into wordly methods. Once or twice I did that but no fruit resulted. Having made the transition into the Kingdom methods my flurries back into worldly methods were useless.

3. Confrontation (a)

Our separation demands:

> 'let us cleanse ourselves from all defilement of flesh and spirit, perfecting holiness in the fear of God.'
>
> (2 Corinthians 7:1)

Separation may lead to confrontation. In my business, when a client seeks to present his accounts, in an inaccurate way or to reduce, unlawfully, taxes for example, then my separation from the world's methods requires confrontation.

When I know or see that confrontation is about to, or

might arise, prayer is immediately applied to the situation. I pray for protection from backlash, I pray for blessing on my client, I pray for truth to rule. Then I stand firm on the truth and will not bend to pressure.

It is better to lose the business than to lose one's close fellowship with the Lord.

In all businesses and secular work situations there is the likelihood of the need to confront in one way or another. I don't believe we should be looking for confrontation, but there is a strong likelihood of it arising. The world's methods are so different from those of the Kingdom. It is when the worldly way tries to push us into something which breaks our higher law that we have to confront.

Discernment is needed – sometimes it will be better to pray 'Lord let this cup pass from me,' than to confront. Hearing God is important.

4. Confrontation (b)

There is also the confrontation with the powers of spiritual darkness for those who have received the spirit of Christ. Very often we don't even suspect that the problems we experience are from the enemy. Discernment of spirits is one of the gifts of the Holy Spirit, I urge that we seek the Lord and gather from Him discernment. With the discernment we can act, and confront the schemes of the enemy.

In all confrontation it is good to have the strength of the body around you. One of our church members, just a couple of months ago, faced redundancy from one of the major banks. There were four or five brothers together in a prayer group. We discerned that this was an enemy action, trying to rob our brother of his job. Defensive action was taken, binding the activity of the enemy and praying for favour with the bank authorities. The bank's intention was reversed.

The Lord designed us as a body, subject to Himself as head and reliant on one another for mutual support. It is very important to be submitted to one another in a body situation, be it our local church or some other body of believers. Submission does not mean that we take orders from one another – regardless of his or her position in the

154

church. It does mean that matters can be weighed and tested and that support in prayer and practical things can be provided. Standing alone is a vulnerable place, because God's design is for a body and the gifts of the Spirit are distributed amongst the body, not all locked up in one individual.

5. Witness

Another part of fruitfulness is witness. In business, in our jobs, we are witnesses for Christ. We should therefore be the best of people to deal with. We should be a breath of life to people who come across our paths.

Or are we bogged down with the same moods and petulances that affect our neighbours in the world?

Being a witness is being like Jesus, His character being seen in us. This is not the same as witnessing about Jesus – our lives and attitudes will speak more loudly than our words to those around.

The unsaved need to 'see' that Jesus makes all the difference to us and not necessarily hear a stream of words, especially if our lives do not measure up to those words.

One of the points about witness is that it is not always successful. In fact Paul puts it this way:

> '*But thanks be to God, who always leads us in His triumph in Christ, and manifests through us the sweet aroma of the knowledge of Him in every place. For we are a fragrance of Christ to God among those who are being saved and among those who are perishing: to the one an aroma from death to death, to the other an aroma of life to life.*' (2 Corinthians 2:14–16)

Our responsibility is not to convert everyone we meet. In fact, it is only the Holy Spirit who can bring the new birth required. Our responsibility is to be the sweet aroma, which will be life to life in some cases and death to death in others.

We are that sweet aroma as we live and move and have our being in Jesus and as we are changed from glory to glory by the Spirit, putting to death the deeds of our flesh.

In business life we have a unique opportunity to meet

people who are unbelievers. This gives us the opportunity to reach many folk who would never 'darken' the door of a church. The Full Gospel Businessmen's Fellowship International carries a particular anointing from God to save and heal people. I have found it easy to invite people I meet in business to a dinner or breakfast meeting – 'come to hear a man's life story, no preaching guaranteed, you may well experience a miracle.' Many times I've had the pleasure of seeing people I've taken along saved or healed and I recommend FGBMFI to you very strongly.

We should expect opportunities to witness; divine appointments. They don't always appear convenient, as Douglas shares in his testimony, but then we are here for the Lord's purposes not our own. It is always a great joy when someone is really benefited by our witness.

6. Sonship

I was visiting a businessman contact at his home office one day and was surprised to find his young son at home laid out on the couch. He was ill and had been off school for a number of weeks. As we dealt with our business, I was becoming more and more certain that God did not want me to leave without praying for the boy.

Asking for his father's permission, which was granted, I gently laid my hand on the young lad and prayed for him to be healed. I 'phoned the next day to see if he was alright only to find that he had recovered completely and gone to school.

A son can speak with the authority of the Father, once the Father has given him that right. Jesus started His ministry at 30 years of age and restricted His activity to doing what he saw and heard the Father doing. In the terms of our sonship, God, by the Spirit, anoints us with giftings, expecting and hoping that we will operate in those giftings as we see and hear from Him.

Part of the fruit is learning to be an obedient son, one who can operate in the gifts given by God at His direction, listening to Him rather than presuming to act, acting on instruction rather than impulse or from external pressure.

Maybe it sounds like an unobtainable calling but actually,

like so many things in the Christian life, it is attained step by step. We seem to progress and then fall, to get it right and then wrong. It is all a process of learning and if we are learning, we should be getting better and better.

There is no condemnation when we miss the mark. Rather, the Father would want us to repent, acknowledging our failure, and then go on again.

As Christians we are entrusted with the oracles of God and with the power of God. Both are powerful and can be applied to great fruitfulness.

7. *Living sacrifices*

Paul urges us to present our bodies as living and holy sacrifices. As we were bought with a price, God is entitled to demand this of us. He is kind and gentle however, leading us on by love rather than by applying force.

He is looking for us to come more and more into agreement with the way He sees things. The reward is a closer and closer walk with Him and help in times of need.

Part of my testimony would be to say that more and more I see deliverance from circumstances at the hand of God. More and more I love Him and seek Him and want Him to reveal Himself to me. I have learnt that He knows better than I all about me and my family and business.

Often it is hard on the flesh for the reasons we have already seen – the opposition between the flesh and the spirit. It is like exercise. Exercise is a discipline, which takes effort and the body does not like it. Yet it brings a harvest of physical fitness. How much more should we be exercised in the spiritual realm.

'Bodily discipline is of little profit, but godliness is profitable for all things, since it holds promise for the present life and also for the life to come.' (1 Timothy 4:8)

Our aim is to be like Him, to show His likeness and character – to be godly in all that we do.

157

8. *Beside still waters*

How are we going to achieve this high calling? Really the answer is that we are never going to achieve it at all. Rather, He is going to achieve it in us the more we abide in Him.

Jesus wants us to be led by Him beside still waters and into green pastures (Psalm 23). What an idyllic picture of relaxed grazing this is.

The way to this position is through abiding in Him and Him abiding in us, as outlined in John 15.

Abiding in Jesus is a question of living Spirit-filled life, moving and having our being in the Spirit God so graciously gives. When His Spirit is poured out, the wilderness becomes a fertile field. The righteous will abide in the fertile field and the work of the righteous will be peace and their service quietness and confidence forever and the people will live in a peaceful habitation (from Isaiah 32:15–16).

> 'He who walks righteously, and speaks with sincerity, he who rejects unjust gain, and shakes his hand so they hold no bribe, he who stops his ears from hearing about bloodshed, and shuts his eyes from evil ... He will dwell upon the heights; his refuge will be the impregnable rock; his bread will be given him; his water will be sure.'
>
> (Isaiah 33:15–16)

Chapter 17

Future Prospects

The desire to know the future is not only a fact of life but also a substantial industry! It is not surprising therefore that businessmen should also want to know what the future holds.

In fact, one of the most common business management tools is the budget, which records future expectations. When combined with management accounts which compare the actual result to the forecast it is indeed a useful tool.

The future of my working life will be affected by the overall business climate and by the specific work load that comes my way. So we will look at the future climate first and then the specific loading that we can expect.

What can one say about the future from the perspective of God's Kingdom and how does that affect business matters?

We can look at two aspects of spiritual analysis as follows:

Future prospects – prophetic

> 'Yet once more I will shake not only the earth but also the heaven, and this expression, "yet once more," denotes the removing of those things which can be shaken, as of created things, in order that those things which cannot be shaken may remain.'   (Hebrews 12:26–27)

Everywhere within the Body of Christ we are being told that God is declaring a shaking of this world. It is the prophetic utterance of the day. The current worldwide economic problems are laid at the door of this statement as are virtually all problems – AIDS, famine, war, revolution etc. etc.

Added to the warnings regarding shaking are the increasing proclamations of the imminent return of our Lord Jesus Christ. What are we to understand from all this?

Whether it is imminent or not, we are exhorted to live in the glorious hope of His return –

> *'Live sensibly, righteously and godly in the present age, looking for the blessed hope and glorious appearing of our great God and Saviour, Christ Jesus.'* (Titus 2:13)

One of the tests of the degree to which we love the Lord is found in this expectation. Do we really want the Lord to return now? Or are there other priorities? If we are really in love with Him, then absolutely nothing will stand in the way and we will, together with the Spirit, say, 'Come Lord Jesus.'

Boom and bust foretold

I have been struck by the vision received by David Wilkerson and written in his book, *The Vision*. In the very first few paragraphs he foretells of increasing economic difficulty in the western economies and Japan resulting in massive unemployment after a false economic boom.

ICCC (The International Christian Chamber of Commerce) has received similar warnings. A prophecy given to the founder, Gunnar Olsen, tells of an economic storm breaking loose, whilst God shakes the world to reveal the Kingdom which cannot shake.

My own expectations are of a gradually imploding world economic scene – there will be some ups and downs along the way, but overall trends will be adverse. I expect this to develop into some dramatic reversals, the collapse of one or more major currencies and for it to culminate in the complete collapse of the economic system at some future point. Whether this is months, or years or decades away I do not know, but if pressed on the question I am thinking in terms of a few years.

Future prospects – biblical

One must always weigh the prophetic against the scriptural and be able to find agreement rather than conflict.

This is not the place for a thorough examination of the various interpretations of the future, so I will select the main points.

The book of Revelation carries in chapters 6 to 18 a series of judgements over the earth, the scale and effect of which are enormous and horrific. Certainly we have not yet seen anything to compare with the matters foretold in those pages. (One should say that not all the information in those chapters is judgemental or entirely futuristic – some is background information.)

Chapter 19 foretells a return to earth of the Lord and His armies and chapter 20 a millenial rule of the Lord Himself.

In this brief overview, regardless of the specific interpretations applied, we can see a scenario of shaking which agrees with the prophetic message being delivered to the Church today.

There is a great deal more to say about End Times matters, the rise of antichrist and the economic system to come, but consider it beyond the scope of this book.

How should we think of the future?

We have already seen that we should fix our hope on the glorious return of Jesus. So far as our expectations are concerned we can say with Paul,

> *'For to me, to live is Christ, and to die is gain.'*
> (Philippians 1:21)

The future **should not** be a matter of anxiety or concern for we are commanded not to be anxious, rather to cast our anxieties on Him.

The Lord wants His children to love Him and to love Him far above everything else. Whether we live in great abudance or close to the breadline. He wants our love and He is able to provide for our needs (see Matthew 6:25–34).

Our future thinking should be orientated to bearing fruit, for the time is short. No longer should we think in primarily economic terms, not that we ignore this area, but we should no longer give it the priority it has held in business and in our lives.

What should we do about it?

> *'Therefore having these promises, beloved, let us cleanse ourselves from all defilement of flesh and spirit, perfecting holiness in the fear of God.'*   (2 Corinthians 7:1)

Clean before God, we can boldly come before Him in every time of need. We will need to do this both for ourselves and for each other. We need to live in close fellowship with our Lord. The alternative is to rely on our own abilities and devices in a world of increasing emnity and strife, without divine help.

Our personal walk

We also need to remind ourselves that whatever the overall situation God is able to look after us. In business, for example, the work we need is easy to God. It may well be impossible to us, but to God it is no problem.

The prophecy given to ICCC and referred to earlier contains great hope:

> 'This is the time when this new thing shall be done. It is a plantation which is clean and pure. I see great trees and many smaller trees and bushes. The big trees will protect the plantation when the storm is breaking loose. This is a shelter for many people. No one will be able to touch what I am now doing. The enemies will try to destroy, but I will hit them on their fingers. They will

not succeed. Here is neither high nor low – only Jesus.
The Lord will use these for many miracles. The trees
and bushes are full of fruit and berries containing great
power.

When people see what I am doing, they will envy you,
but they will not be able to enter in. The Lord is show-
ing the kingdom which cannot be shaken. He will send it
down to all those who believe that the Lord is faithful
and real, already here. It shall not be capable of being
shaken here on earth.

Do not let what I am doing rock you out of balance. I
will do unusual things. Just remain calm and in peace.
All the answers come from Me. You can trust Me completely. Do not trust in flesh and blood. Yield yourselves to Me and lean on Me. Keep your eyes on the
kingdom that cannot shake – that begins here – that the
Lord sends to all those who hold Him for faithful. It
begins already here and shall not be taken away from
you.

It shall not be taken away from the Lord's people and
will remain when Jesus comes. It shall not be capable of
being shaken here on earth.'

God is faithful and true

This is the issue – are we counting God as faithful and true?
Are we relying upon Him? Are we walking in close fellowship? Is Jesus actually Lord and lover?

As we ponder these questions and consider that the future
will bring perilous times, we can know that we have the great
counsellor to help us. We can and should be calling upon the
Holy Spirit to lead us into all truth and to change us more
and more into the likeness of Jesus.

What of my future?

Well, I am content to leave that in the hands of my Father. I
have learnt to trust Him and I know He loves and cares for
me. I will remain in the place of my calling, only changing if

He so directs. In that place I shall expect to bear fruit and shall expect God to meet all my needs – just as He promises through the Word, for He is faithful and true.

What about your future?

It is my hope that what is written here will help you. I believe that the Lord has led me to recognise the principles by which we should live. The next chapter gives you a chance for some self-assessment.

I wish you every success and blessing as you walk through life with your Lord and Saviour, exhorting you to love Him more and more.

Are You Spiritually Solvent?

Does your spiritual balance sheet add up?

Here is a chance to find out. There follow seven statements regarding the application of faith in the working life. For each statement you score yourself on a scale from −3 to +3.

If you thoroughly agree with the statement and are applying it in your life, then score +3.

If you agree but are only partially working it out, then score +1 or +2.

If you are far from understanding the point and definitely not working it out, then score −3.

In this way you grade yourself on each point.

It is possible that you will end up with a minus score and that is part of the objective of the exercise.

The maximum score is +21 and the minimum −21.

Statement 1

You are not your own, you were bought with a price – therefore you have no right to decide your own destiny. The contract for the sale was completed when you believed in Jesus – but this contract is a love contract and not forced upon us. Love (*agape*) is love involving the choice of the will, which God demonstrated in allowing Jesus to be crucified for us. Love (*phileo*) is friendship love. God has both for us and expects us to have both for Him.

Question: Is Jesus Lord in your life and do you really love Him; I mean really love Him?

Score ☐

Statement 2

What do you think of 'The Truth'? Is your life and business activity built on the truth?

In Matthew 7 we read of the wise and the foolish builders – both hear the word of God and the storms rage against both. The one built on truth survives. Are you setting aside the truth in order to keep to traditions? For example, many businessmen squeeze their creditors as much as possible, or borrow to their limit, or suppress the work force in terms and conditions.

Question: Are you building on solid rock by doing what you know God requires from His voice and the Scriptures?

Score ☐

Statement 3

Motive. We are expected by God to have only one motive or ambition and that, to please Him. This is achieved by walking the way Jesus walked – He did what He saw and heard His Father doing.

The grass can always appear greener in another job or another business. Is your motive to obey Him where you are now? The motive to make money for the Kingdom sounds good but has God Himself asked you to do that? If not, the result is doomed to failure.

Question: What is your motive? Apply honesty to your score!

Score ☐

Statement 4

There is one 'anointed place' in which you are called to be working. God has prepared for each *'good works for us to walk in'* (Ephesians 2:10). We are told to stay in the calling we were in when saved and to change direction by hearing God speak to us. He speaks and we obey. Sometimes we change by force of circumstances and not voluntarily – in such cases submit the circumstances to God, bind the enemy and go with the flow in the certain knowledge that God will bring good out of the situation. In the anointed place you can boldly ask the Father in prayer, knowing that you are in His will.

Question: Are you in your 'anointed place'?

Score

Statement 5

Are you led by the Spirit? Are you walking a life of faith? Faith has two aspects. A passive aspect, which says, 'I have trust in God and confidence in His character and His word which give me security and certainty in life.' An active aspect which hears God speak specifically and acts accordingly in various situations.

Question: How are you on both the passive and active elements of faith?

Score

Statement 6

God blesses and prospers His children with every blessing and desires good for them.

Question: How is your thinking? Do you think that God is unlikely to bless you? After all, you are not worthy, you don't deserve it. Or are you a 'son of God', unworthy but made worthy, unrighteous but made righteous?

Is your mind renewed and continuously renewed in the truth?

Score ☐

Statement 7

1. The enemy comes to rob, kill and destroy. Your working life, your job prospects, your relationships – in fact, anything he can get his hands on.
2. Praise is a powerful tool which enthrones God and has the power to see us through circumstances. Rejoice in the Lord always and again I say rejoice. Praise, deliberate praise in adverse circumstances is powerful.
3. God loves a cheerful giver. Not a question of paying debts but generously giving as He directs by His voice.

Questions:
1. Are you defending your business life from enemy activity?
2. Are you positive, even abundant in praise when circumstances and your flesh scream the opposite?
3. Are you giving generously?

Score ☐

How about your total?

How have you scored? Add your seven scores together.

Total Score ☐

Well, how did you do? Are you solvent? Is there room for improvement?

Over to you to seek the Lord about the weak areas and to build yourself up in the faith.

Taped versions of a presentation covering the spiritual balance sheet are available from:

ICCC Tapes
Jeremy Welby
Church End House
Whichford
Shipston on Stour
Warwickshire CV36 5PG

The study lasts approximately 45 minutes and the tape costs £2.50 (cheques payable to 'ICCC').

A list of other taped studies covering many aspects of the working life is available from the same address.

Testimonies

I have asked a few of my Christian friends to provide a short testimony to the work of God in and through their lives.

My friends are business people, either in employment or running their own business. Their business interests vary from painter/decorator to Rolls Royce and Bentley dealer, from headhunting to kitchen design and renewal.

They have in common a personal relationship with my best friend – Jesus Christ. Like me, they have found Him to be a constant source of love and strength, the first port of call in times of need, and The One who is able to affect circumstances even in the realm of business.

The point of including these testimonies – and many, many more could have been included – is to demonstrate that Jesus is interested in every part of our lives including our work; that He has the power to direct us into fruitful labour and that He is able to come to our aid when things press against us.

Chris Hill

It was May 1981 and I was walking towards a bar with a business colleague in New Orleans, when someone walked in front of me, looked me straight in the face and asked 'Do you know my friend Jesus?' No sooner had he spoken the words than he was nowhere to be seen: nowhere to be seen on a straight and quiet road!

During that same trip whilst seated in the aircraft waiting to take off, the pilot announced a delay of half an hour. While we were patiently waiting, a choir, who, unknown to us, were travelling on the same plane, broke into song with 'Do you know my friend Jesus?'

For those who have had similar experiences, it will come as no surprise to hear that back home my wife was praying, 'Lord, send angels across his path.'

It was some two years later that I made a commitment to Jesus. I had resisted, having felt the prompting on previous occasions, but each time my mind would give me some apparently good reason not to respond.

I had not come from a religious background, although I had always believed in God. But there is a big difference between believing that God exists and knowing the God who was and is and will always be. What finally prompted me to actively believe in this God was the evidence of His working, seeing Him heal the incurable during a healing service at a church in Leicestershire in 1982. Having made that decision and commitment, things moved fast.

For me there were no flashing lights or trumpets, but there was a gentle assurance that something had changed and as I moved in faith, God moved.

It must have been within the first six months of asking Jesus into my life that I found myself in a prayer group with other businessmen praying for the opening for a Full Gospel Businessmen's Fellowship Chapter to be formed in Northamptonshire. Within no time the opportunity arose and the Chapter started, immediately flourishing. In what seems like no time at all my lifestyle, beliefs, motivation and vision were completely transformed.

Perhaps one of the greatest transformations was in the

area of work. Having moved from Essex to North-amptonshire with a change of employer in 1978, I found myself working in a company headed by a man who openly professed to be a Christian. Some four years later, after making a commitment myself, it was good to be able to share together our faith in Christ. Later in 1988 and now a Director of that same company, we were acquired by a competitor and this resulted in many changes and a period of much uncertainty. This was a perfect opportunity to draw closer to the Lord.

My wife and I prayed about what we should do. My new employer had offered me a good position with a substantial increase in salary and excellent future prospects, but a move south was required and weekends spent in house-hunting had proved fruitless.

In the August of 1987, the owner of a Japanese business with whom I had had contact for many years met with me in London. The suggestion arose that we form a business together to market his products in the UK. The following week I took a week's holiday and spent it in Japan. On returning to the UK I resigned but a restrictive covenant prevented me from working in the same industry for six months. I left with a golden handshake but no work to go to – I was in effect unemployed.

It was now the beginning of January and my wife and I formed a Consultancy – within one week we had a six month contract! This proved crucial. The golden handshake I had received was needed for share capital and the consultancy contract provided for our living costs. Without that income it would have been difficult. Not one penny of that share capital was touched.

In June 1988 I received a 'phone call from a company I had never heard of and a person I did not know. A ten minute meeting discussing a product that I was unable to demonstrate because it had not yet been produced, resulted in my first order worth £66,000 for the business I had formed, to commence on 1st July.

Some people can call these things coincidences. I cannot. Having a marketing background, I know only too well how difficult it is to promote yourself and your company with a view to locating potential buyers. To have a potential customer contact you in your home when there had been no promotion whatsoever is almost beyond belief. But with God all things are possible to those who believe.

The development of our company has been punctuated with such instances that can only really be put down to the intervention of God and his continual faithfulness. Not all such experiences have been entirely welcome. For example: having agreed at the outset that we would never borrow money – and we haven't – I realised towards the end of 1992 that some of my faith had been transferred from faith in God to faith in a positive cash flow. The Bible tells us clearly that we cannot serve two masters; also that the love of money (not money itself) is the root of all evil. Maybe a scriptural principle that is particularly relevant in these turbulent times is this: everything that we can see is temporary, what we cannot see is eternal. We can see money in the physical sense, in a bank statement, in an invoice, but we know how temporary it can be in terms of its value, its power and its resultant interest. In fact, everything that we can buy with it is of interest until we have it and then familiarity so often brings contempt.

The thought of being without God today is terrifying to me. The desire to know Him better and to walk closer with Him increases almost daily.

There was a time when I couldn't see the relevance of Christianity and Jesus in life generally and in the business life in particular. Over countless centuries prophets of doom have spoken about the end of the world and the destruction of the earth. Most of the speculation has borne little relevance to biblical truth, but the Bible clearly tells us that we will not know the exact time of Christ's return, but we will recognise the signs.

Until recently some of the most significant biblical prophecies related to the End Times had not taken place and so much speculation in the past could not have had much relevance to the life of those living in former generations. However, today some of the key signs listed by Jesus in Matthew

24 and Luke 21 can all be seen happening. One of the most important of these is the restoration of the Jews to their homeland in 1948 and their subsequent control of Jerusalem following the Six Day War of 1967.

With the present turmoil in the world political, ethnic and religious structures, it doesn't take a lot of difficulty to believe that perhaps now is the time that God is shaking all things!

What better time could there be to be standing on the Rock that can never be shaken! (Matthew 7:24–25).

Katrina Moss

I would like to think that I involve God in every area of my work life, but if I am really honest, the main time He gets my full attention is when I am in trouble. I am sure as I progress with my relationship with God that this will change, but isn't it great to know that, wherever we are, whether we feel we are in credit or overdrawn with God, it makes no difference to Him? He still loves us and looks for opportunities to show He is interested in everything we do and for situations where He can demonstrate how much He cares for us. I am so glad that my relationship with God is based on His grace and mercy towards me, not on what I can or cannot achieve through hard work and effort.

One of the first times I really let God have an input into my business was at the end of November 1990. I run a franchise for a kitchen door replacement company called RE-NU, where, instead of ripping out everything and starting again from scratch, we fit made-to-measure doors and drawers onto customer's existing units, which saves them time, money and mess. As Christmas approaches, everybody wants their 'new-look' kitchen installed in time for all the cooking and the admiring comments of assembled families. This particular year I had been very busy and had promised too many people that their kitchens would be fitted before Santa came down the chimney. I was at that time a dreadful worrier and hated to let customers down under any circumstances. I had carefully gone through the diary and knew that there were more days' work than there were days in December. Who was I going to let down? How would they react, after I had promised them? I woke up every morning, feeling physically sick with worry – there was no solution to the problem, or was there? I remembered about that time two particular scriptures, both in Matthew's Gospel:

> *'Therefore do not worry about tomorrow, for tomorrow will worry about itself. Each day has enough trouble of its own.'* (Matthew 6:34)

> *'Come to me, all you who are weary and burdened, and I will give you rest. Take my yoke upon you and learn from me, for I am gentle and humble in heart, and you will find rest for your souls. For my yoke is easy and my burden is light.'* (Matthew 11:28–29)

So God was telling me not to worry and that He wanted my burdens. Well, that was great in theory, but how would it work in practice? I sat at my desk and told Him what the problem was and that no-one ever decided they wanted to leave it until after Christmas, but that I was going to trust Him to sort it out for me. Every morning it became a battle, as I still felt sick and my chest was tight, but I made the choice every day to believe that God was going to accomplish the impossible. Days went past where nothing happened, but still I went on trusting in God and in His word. Then, my fitter started to complete jobs that would normally have taken three to four days in two, customers started to ring up and ask if I would mind postponing their kitchens until January, with the result that every single person who wanted their kitchen in before Christmas received it.

Now you could say that was coincidence or circumstance, but I truly believe that my prayer and trusting in God made the difference. I once heard someone say in response to the coincidence theory, that wasn't it funny that when they stopped praying the coincidences stopped!

I became a Christian in January 1990 and I am grateful that God doesn't decide to challenge us in every area of our lives all at once – I know I couldn't cope with it. But He treats us all as individuals and deals with us at a pace that is right for us. I find that my conscience and my views on certain moral issues are quite different now from those I held most of my adult life to date.

I was in a situation where something I had done regularly for years, I knew God was telling me was unacceptable behaviour. The fact that everyone does it, justifies it to yourself, but carries **no** weight with God. I decided that I was going to do my utmost to make sure that I was no longer guilty of this action. The only problem was that someone else was involved who couldn't see my point of view, or God's. I tried to explain that I now felt differently and was not prepared to go against my conscience, which resulted in quite a scene. Often, when you are with a non-Christian, going against the flow, especially when there are financial implications, it can be difficult, but with some effort on my part I stood my ground and explained my reasons. The day after this incident I had **five** customers ring up wanting to place orders – in all the years of running this business, this has never happened in one day. I know it was God's grace that He honoured my step and it spoke volumes to the other person involved.

Grace is one of those words I often heard, but didn't really think about its true meaning. It means 'unmerited favour' and I have certainly been on the receiving end of plenty of that. My business was going through a particularly slow patch in spring 1992, which is unusual as spring is normally one of my busiest times of year, but I had just put it down to the general economic climate, as other franchises were also doing badly. I went along to a meeting of ICCC, where we were able to share about our different circumstances and they prayed for my business, that God would bless it. In the following few days, I received more than my monthly target for sales!

The problem with the Great Unpaid Troubleshooter is you never know how He is going to answer your prayers or when. Sometimes it is quick, and recently I had a very unexpected and supersonic quick answer to prayer. The franchisor who owned my particular franchise, although not

totally dishonest, was, I felt beginning to use business prac-
tices that I was very unhappy about. I myself, did not follow
his example, but felt that I was tainted with the same brush,
by association. I wanted to distance myself from him, but
was tied to a contract which would prevent me from trading
if I did not continue with him. I also explained that there was
one particular person in the group whom I really respected
and liked, the person who owned the factory.

I brought this matter to the attention of the ICCC prayer
group and they asked that God would speak to me clearly
and deal with the matter. The next day I had a meeting with
the franchisor and the top franchisees in the company to
discuss marketing strategies for the whole group. So you can
imagine, that when the meeting started and we were told
that the agenda had been changed because the franchisor
had a closure order against him, I was absolutely stunned.
This meant that my contract would now be null and void,
allowing me to trade independently, if I so wished. During a
break for coffee I ran down the hotel corridor, just thanking
God! I could hardly believe what was happening – we had
only prayed the night before! God is able to work in ways we
cannot imagine, we just need to trust Him. He also pays
attention to every detail, for the person who eventually took
over the franchise was the person I mentioned whom I really
trusted and respected.

This last year has probably been one of the most difficult
years of my working life – I have experienced more problems
in one six-month period than in all my previous years of
trading put together. I prayed to God for help, troubleshoot-
ing, strength, wisdom, etc., and, although some prayers
were answered, their outcome just seemed to make the
situation worse. How could God allow me to be put under
such stress in all the areas where I was most weak? Where
was God when I really needed Him? He was there all the
time – I remember someone telling me that He never lets us
be tested beyond what we can bear. That was sometimes
very difficult to believe, but I held on, even though I felt as if
I was going to fall. Now, looking back over this period some
nine months further on, I can see that God did answer my

prayers, but not in the way I had expected. He decided not to sort out my problems, but to develop my character, so that I would have the skills to enable me to cope with areas that habitually I have found difficult. I can't say it was a pleasant experience, but I am thankful to God that He loves me and always has my best interests at heart. I really appreciate the fact that God is always faithful to me, even when I am not faithful to Him.

I would like our relationship to change from Unpaid Troubleshooter and Boss to that of Partners, God being the Senior Partner with me as His willing and trusted Junior Partner.

John Patrick

I am now in the 29th year of my working life, having graduated in 1964 from Durham University and joined Shell as a graduate trainee. Since then I have worked for a Swiss pharmaceutical company, nine years with the Commonwealth Development Corporation, followed by a move into recruitment when I joined Coopers and Lybrand to recruit qualified staff for 30 overseas countries. Then, wishing to see if I could become a general manager, I ran a subsidiary of an American company, who have 6,000 staff in the Middle East and I was responsible for recruiting all grades of medical and technical staff from the UK into Saudi Arabia and the Gulf. This came to an end in 1984 when we lost a contract worth over $1 billion and I found myself firstly making my staff redundant and then, around three months later, I became redundant myself.

At that point I joined my present company, which is a major international management consultancy, where I am senior consultant in recruitment (known in the trade as a head-hunter).

Until six years ago Christianity was really not part of my life at all, other than that seven years after I married my wife, Tricia became a Christian. I skilfully managed not to get involved in that, but concentrated on my new career as a consultant, where I soon found I had the right profile and was successful. Unfortunately, success also meant increased stress as, for the first time in my life, it was almost like running my own solo business within the company, with virtually no back-up if I was sick or had too many assignments on at any one time. This ultimately resulted in a classic case of burn-out, when I found myself in the middle of the night stretched out on the landing paralysed and unable to move. Miraculously my wife woke up, dragged me back to bed and, after 10–15 minutes, I gradually regained the use of my limbs. Two days of rest followed and then I returned to the office.

This first physical warning was followed quite shortly by a spiritual warning. While commuting home from Waterloo to Guildford, someone next to me (who was probably only five to ten years older than myself) choked on a sweet, triggering a heart attack. Despite the almost immediate attentions of two nurses and then a doctor, he was declared dead and removed from the train! As the burn-out had challenged my physical and, to some extent, mental condition, this was the first challenge to my spiritual perception of death and what might happen thereafter.

The ultimate spiritual challenge was not long in coming: I had a dream where I met with Jesus in a desert (probably representative of my spiritual life at that time) and He took me up into an open glass-sided lift through a building where people were oblivious of this, working away and concentrating on their own lives. He then took me up to the top of a mountain and showed me a beautiful, green and pleasant land and communicated to me the word 'love' with the accompaniment of an incredible feeling quite unlike anything I had experienced before, but which I would now describe as being like the baptism in the Spirit. It was not long after this at a Full Gospel Businessmen's dinner that I was powerfully convicted by the Holy Spirit, committed myself to the Lord and so arrived at the office the next day as a new Christian.

Immediately it was clear to me that God was interested in my business, although I didn't know that this was taught in Scripture. I quickly realised that it was necessary to pray and ask for help and guidance through the Holy Spirit, who is the only consultant who really knows all the answers. From the very start I could see His hand on the assignments that came to me. My first experience of his intervention was on an assignment that I had been working on for at least twelve months and where I had put up many good candidates, but none of them had accepted an offer to join the company in question. Every candidate who looked keen, at the last moment withdrew. The last straw appeared to be a perfect candidate, who was married with a young family, and was being offered an extra £10,000 per annum with much better prospects. He too had decided not to accept. Not long afterwards, my American client told me that he had himself found someone and had appointed him. Although I was pleased for the client, it was an obvious disappointment and I wondered what God was doing in all this. About six weeks later, I was contacted by the candidate with the young family, who told me that my client had just closed the whole of the UK operation with a loss of all the jobs and I saw that God had protected me and had not allowed me to take a candidate out of a secure job into almost immediate redundancy.

My results for the company in this first two years continued to be excellent and I had many opportunities to witness to colleagues and clients. This all changed in 1990 when very suddenly my monthly billing went down to zero. It seemed to be a time to stand in faith, to praise God in all things, to earnestly seek the Lord to see what He was trying to say to me and what areas of my life He needed to sort out. This period in the wilderness contrasted with my colleagues, who were in boom times and probably the extent of my witness during that period was to try to keep cheerful and to try to keep trusting in God for all things. I was able to sort out various areas in my life that the Lord pointed out to me, but still no business came in and I began to feel the cold fear of redundancy hovering over me. Then God began to reveal to me the necessity of praying with my wife and so receiving her full support and love. Together we sought the Lord to open the channels, but still nothing came. At this time, whilst praying one morning, I received a very clear word from the Lord about future work and it was that He would give me the National Health Service as a 'garden' to work in. I wrote this down, but, as nothing happened within a week or even a few months, I forgot about it. In the meantime, the first small bit of work came from an old client and them amazingly, work returned to previous levels just as the recession started to bite and the workload of my colleagues started going in the wrong direction!

Since then I have had two record years where the Lord has taught me about my needs, including some difficult decisions on new assignments that came in. I knew that my needs had been met and that I had to give these assignments away to others. God is a God of abundance.

Two years ago and six months after the specific word about the National Health Service, unexpectedly and with no track record, I was asked to carry out one of the biggest jobs in the NHS to find the new Chief Executive of St Thomas's Hospital. Since then I have handled the recruitment of a further six Chief Executive posts within the NHS.

I find that, as the effects of the recession shake, not only my employer, but also most of my clients, many more executives and managers are realising that they cannot control all the rapidly changing factors in their business with any certainty, despite professionalism, training and endless amounts of hard work. While there is still incredulity when one describes how God works in supernatural ways in business through prayer, I find that they are now prepared to listen more readily and even some non-Christians are happy to accept prayer for themselves and their work.

It will always be a spiritual battleground as the stakes are very high and for too long the kingdom of darkness has controlled much of the business world. But more Christians are entering the battle, realising their authority in Christ and the power of both family and corporate prayer within the work arena. This is a difficult and testing walk, but it is a rewarding one, for only businesses based on Kingdom principles can hope to survive and provide and feed those in need in the future.

Douglas Rotberg

My name is Douglas Rotberg. I am Managing Director of a Rolls Royce and Bentley dealership in Surrey.

Let me begin by giving you a testimony of someone whom I knew very well indeed. He was a Rolls Royce Bentley owner. He was a self-made man who left school at the age of fifteen with no qualifications whatsoever. This man was extremely aggressive and he clawed his way up through business and by the age of 35 he had made a lot of money. He used to drive around in a Rolls Royce and smoke a big Havana cigar. He had, in fact, a very high profile lifestyle – gambling, horses and so on. He was married. His personal life was an absolute mess! He suffered terribly with depression. To everybody else, he looked like the man everybody wanted to be, but he was suicidal and became an alcoholic. In fact, one day he collapsed with alcoholic poisoning. He was a man with a tremendous temper. He used to throw desks across rooms at his staff. He was quite a handful! In fact he used to get through staff like confetti. He really was not a very nice person. I remember talking to a friend who said that he went round to see him once for lunch – he just popped in to see him, but he wouldn't see him because he hadn't actually made an appointment. He would not see anybody at any time of night or day unless they had made an appointment to see him.

Now, that guy about three years ago drove his car up to a tent in East Grinstead, Sussex. He parked and went into that tent, but the interesting part is that he didn't come out. Inside was a Billy Graham meeting and that day he gave his life to the Lord. That person was actually me. How it came about is a very long story, but in brief. I had a secretary who was a Christian. She was a back-slidden Christian who had recently come back to the Lord and she could actually see what was driving me – and it was driving me – and she and her family earnestly prayed for me. I had really no idea that this was going on. Before the Billy Graham meeting she asked me to go to church and, under duress, one day I went to church and enjoyed it, but I didn't let her know. She kept on and on about Billy Graham and, without her knowing, that Friday I decided to go to a meeting as I knew she wouldn't be in that particular tent. That day, I met with the living God – I was on my hands and knees and I was in tears.

Today my past life has gone. That woman is now my wife. We are a Christian family. We have two children and I am a totally different man. But, having said I gave my life to the Lord, all you who have done this will know that giving every part of life to the Lord is a process that takes a long time. My personal life I gladly gave to Him because it was in such a mess. The Lord just got in there and really sorted it out. When it comes to giving your business away – that's when I really stumbled, because as I saw it, I had made that business, it was my company and I had built it up. So I was a Christian on a Sunday but on Monday I was back in the world. I find that the Lord takes me to areas where I have to make a yes or no decision and my business nearly went into receivership three times before I actually gave it to the Lord. The last time I thought I was going down for £30,000 and I just said 'Right, Lord, it's yours. I am going to walk away from it. If you want me back here, then you make the company liquid and I'll go back and I'll run it for you.' They found an error in the accounting amounting to £32,000, so we were actually £2,000 in profit. From that day, I went back to work for Douglas Daniels Ltd as their Managing Director. The Lord is my Chairman and I listen, or hopefully listen, to what he tells me to do.

It seems a strange business for a Christian to be involved in: selling Rolls Royce cars. When I first gave my life to the Lord, I said 'Surely I'm in the wrong business, Lord. Here I am dealing with people who adore these vehicles. It's what they live and strive for.' But in my small time working for the Lord, He keeps putting people in my office, giving me opportunity to speak to people who would otherwise have no Christian contact. I just thank the Lord, firstly for providing for me and, secondly for the people he brings in to see me, because everything that I have comes from the Lord. Business has changed with the recession – I used to have a three-week lead time, but now as I open the door on Monday morning, my workshop has got enough work to keep them going for half a day. That happens every Monday, but every Friday, when I look at the timesheets, everybody's been productive. That demonstrates provision coming from the Lord. Often I arrive at the office on Monday morning and someone phones up wanting the exact car that I have in stock. That is nothing to do with me. That is from the Lord. All the time it is coming from my Father and the glory must really go to Him.

Last week I was sitting in my office, desperate to get to a meeting, late as ever, when a friend of mine who is in the estate agency business arrived. He doesn't know the Lord, but he came into the office and said, 'Doug, where is it all going to end?' I thought, 'Lord, come on, you don't really mean this do you?' and He said 'Yes!' So we sat down and I shared the word with him for two hours. It is vital to hear what the Father's saying to you, because your business is not the most important thing. The most important thing is to spread the Good News of Jesus in the business circle. Now it is my firm belief that the Lord is calling Christian business people to stand up and be counted. He is building a strong army of Christian business people. I want to encourage you that the Lord is wanting to work in each and every one of your lives in a very strong and powerful way. I have seen people lose fortunes overnight! Gone! People like that are desperate. They will turn to Christians and say, 'What's going on, where is it all coming from?' We must have the strength to tell them about Jesus, to tell them how He affects our lives, how He is running our businesses.

Charles Underwood

As a qualified graphic artist, I had made a sideways step to become a printing machine minder. After a period of seven and a half years, I ended up hating the job with a passion! It was during this time of despondency that fellow Christians at the Full Gospel Businessmen's Fellowship International spent a number of meetings praying for me. Finally, my employer asked if I would find myself another job.

My wife discussed my situation with a well-respected

friend who suggested that I became a painter and decorator. This was the last employment I could visualise myself in, so, unsure as to whether this was God's leading, my wife and I asked for his confirmation. Shortly afterwards, at a FGBMFI dinner meeting, a lady sitting opposite me looked across the table and, without knowing any of the circumstances, said 'You're just the person to decorate my hall,' So, being unemployed, I apprehensively agreed to carry out the work, asking God to confirm that this was His leading by bringing in more work. Next came a request from my sister to paint the exterior of her house, then two of her neighbours asked me to paint their houses also!

It was at this stage that I decided to seek advice from Peter Michell, a Christian friend and accountant. He counselled us and, sensing God was in it, he advised us to 'go with it and see where God leads.' He showed my wife how to organise the book-keeping and things seemed to fall into place. Back in the days when I was operating printing machines, I had often dreamed of being in business for myself and it seemed that God was fulfilling his promise in Psalm 37:4, *'Delight yourself in the Lord and He will give you the desires of your heart.'*

After I had been in business for some while, I reached a stage where I hadn't any work except for one outstanding estimate which was accepted providing I commenced the work two weeks later (after the finish of the World Cup!). Every morning I prayed that God would give me favour with this customer (Psalm 106:4): *'Remember me, O Lord, when you show favour to your people'*). Work commenced and on the second morning my customer gave me several pounds of fresh home-grown gooseberries. A few days later I received several pounds of new potatoes and on completion of the job he gave my wife a box of chocolates, a large bucket of dahlias from his garden and £5 to spend on myself. I certainly received favour! In addition to this, the amount of work from this man's friends and neighbours amounted to over six months' continual employment. The very next customer made a cot quilt for my son (a similar one sold for just under £100 in the local village shop). A friend who had prayed that as one job ended, another would come along, had had his prayer answered.

On another occasion I was contacted by the caretaker of a local office block to ask if I could carry out plumbing. Although fairly major work, this turned out to be relatively easy and in the next two years the client provided me with regular profitable customers. Following a small disagreement with the caretaker, the business stopped. However, I felt it was not a natural problem, but a supernatural one and that the enemy was behind it, in accordance with John 10:10 *'The enemy comes to rob, steal and destroy.'* As I prayed, I felt the Lord telling me to follow the example of Joshua, when he walked round the city of Jericho. I proceeded to walk around the building, claiming the ground as mine. Soon afterwards there was a change of Managing Director and House Manager, so I wrote to them thanking them for their custom in the past and offering my services in the future. As a result the customer returned and has continued to provide many thousands of pounds of business.

As I look back, I realise that God has done a tremendous thing: when I was a child, I used to try to decide what sort of work I really wanted to do when I grew up and it seemed that what would really suit me would be to be able to work out of doors in the summer, but inside in the winter. Amazingly this is just what I am now able to do!

How to Become a Christian

Maybe you have read this book and would like to know how to become a Christian – so here is a simple guide.

Step 1: Recognise the need

You may already recognise that you need someone to save you from your own sin and failure – if so, go to Step 2.

You may consider that you are a good person, the type who is always willing to help a neighbour and wouldn't hurt a fly. You wouldn't sin; well, not knowingly. However, you probably have not considered just what constitutes sin. Your idea of sin could be limited to that which is right or wrong in your own eyes.

God has laid down His view of sin in the Scripture. God is the judge and He will judge by His declared view not by your view or my view.

If you do not know God you have definitely broken the very first command – to love the Lord your God with all your heart. So, even if you have lived an otherwise perfect life (and you haven't), I am afraid you have fallen at the first hurdle just like every single human being before you.

If you don't love the Lord your God with all your heart you are a sinner.

Step 2: Recognise the solution

'God so loved the world that He gave His only begotten Son, that whoever believes in Him should not perish, but have eternal life.' (John 3:16)

God sent Jesus as an atoning sacrifice to pay the penalty of sin, which the Scripture describes as death, on your behalf.

I should have died as the penalty for my sin and so should you, but God loves me and you and wants our love in response. The only way was for another to bear the just and correct penalty on our behalf. Not just anyone would do, it had to be one who was Himself sinless and Jesus was the only one who could do it.

Jesus is God's Son – He is divine. According to John chapter 1, in the beginning was the Word, and the Word was made flesh and dwelt amongst us.

The solution is Jesus, His death on the cross for our sakes.

Step 3: Accept the Saviour

Jesus' death was not the end of the story. After three days He rose from the dead. He was triumphant – death could not hold Him because He has an eternal, imperishable life. Jesus is alive today and He gives this invitation:

> *'Behold I stand at the door and knock, if anyone hears My voice and opens the door, I will come in to him, and will dine with him and him with Me.'* (Revelation 3:20)

If you want Jesus to enter into your life as your Saviour and Lord this prayer can be your starting place:

> 'Jesus I recognise that I have sinned and fallen short of the glory of God. I see that You are God's Son and that Your death was as a substitute for me. I accept and believe that You have taken my sin on the cross in my place. I now invite You to come in to me just as You say – Jesus please enter and fill me with your Holy Spirit. Amen.'

You have been saved. Ask God to lead you to His people, to the church of His choice for you so that you can grow quickly in the things of God.

Maybe that prayer is too difficult but you do want to know more. Ask God to reveal Himself to you. Speak to Him as if He is there. Ask and keep asking. If you hunger after God you will find Him.

Contact addresses

ICCC – *National Secretary*

>Edwin Smith
>21 Hocombe Road
>Chandlers Ford
>Hants SO5 1SL

FGBMFI – *National Secretary*

>PO Box 11
>Knutsford
>Cheshire WA16 6QP

Author

>Peter Michell
>PO Box 107
>Haywards Heath
>Sussex RH17 6AW